LOST, LOOKING & FOUND

A Literary Salon's Renaissance

EDINBURGH LITERARY SALON

D1368362

-m-
MERCHISTON PUBLISHING
www.merchistonpublishing.com

First published in 2021 by
Merchiston Publishing
Colinton Road, Edinburgh, EH10 5DT
in partnership with
Edinburgh Literary Salon
www.edinburghliterarysalon.org
by MSc Publishing students at Edinburgh Napier University
Katya Bacica, Martha Bradley, Sophie Caldwell, Elise Carmichael, Eilidh Gilmour,
Laura Hunt, Jack Jamieson, Madison Klopfer, Madeleine Mankey, Beth Morris,
Bethany Nelson, Romie Nguyen, Luc Palmer, Emma Scott, Eilidh Sawyers

Cover and Book Design © Merchiston Publishing 2021
Illustrations © James Flowerdew
and Penny Hodson 2021

ISBN: 978-1-911524-01-4

Printed by Bell & Bain Ltd, Glasgow, G46 7UQ
Typeset in Mrs Eaves OT, 12/14

Contents

FOUND

Acknowledgements

We are grateful to the following organisations and individuals for their support and all their work to produce this ground-breaking new book.

The Edinburgh Literary Salon Steering Group.

Edinburgh UNESCO City of Literature Trust.

Baillie Gifford.

The staff (Avril Gray and David McCluskey) and students of Edinburgh Napier University's MSc Publishing programme 2020/21 –

Editorial: Katya Bacica, Laura Hunt, Madison Klopfer, Madeleine Mankey, Bethany Nelson, Luc Palmer, and Eilidh Sawyers.

Marketing: Martha Bradley, Sophie Caldwell, Jack Jamieson, Beth Morris, and Romie Nguyen.

Production: Elise Carmichael, Eilidh Gilmour, and Emma Scott.

Cover: Elise Carmichael and Madeleine Mankey.

The judging panel for blind submissions: Avril Gray, Rebecca Heap, Miriam Johnson, Eleanor Pender, Simon Puttock, Blythe Robertson, and John Stoddart.

Contributors: Ron Butlin, Philip Caveney, Srishti Chaudhary, Regi Claire, Lyndsey Croal, Julie Galante, Joy Hendry, Carola Huttmann, Andrew Jamieson, Jim Mackintosh, Seán Martin, Sadie Maskery, Jen McGregor,

Ricky Monahan Brown, Susan Nickalls, Stuart A. Paterson, Mary Paulson-Ellis, Tracey S. Rosenberg, Natalie Rowland, Sharon Sampson, Devana Senanayake, Sara Sheridan, and Catherine Simpson.

Illustrators: James Flowerdew and Penny Hodson.

Last, but not least, The Wash Bar, where we hope to meet again soon.

Foreword

Travellers in the wilderness of this world

Asking when the Edinburgh Literary Salon began is not a simple question to answer. Was it before the Scott Monument dominated the skyline of Princes Street? Or before they drained the Nor' Loch? Did the Castle yet sit atop the Old Town prow? Or was it not long after Arthur's Seat spewed its guts sideways 350 million years ago, to provide the rock upon which said castle was built? No, perhaps that's too far.

For writers, Edinburgh is a palimpsest; layers of history make up our city. From the castle perched on that volcanic plug, to the inscriptions on pavements, in closes, and the walls of the Parliament Building, this place is richly endowed by the past. To be able to rub the big toe of David Hume, visit the grave of Adam Smith, or doff your bunnet to John Knox pointing to his Bible in St Giles Cathedral (after all, The Kirk pioneered education) – to live in Edinburgh is to live in a city steeped in Enlightenment.

Enlightenment and literature sit side by side. Even those whose relationship with Edinburgh is less intimate may know our main train station is the only one in the world named after a novel. *Waverley*'s author, Sir Walter Scott, is celebrated in The Writers' Museum, along with

Robert Burns and Robert Louis Stevenson. The museum is tucked behind a bar where, once a month, a bunch of writers meet to mingle, blether, drink, debate, and exchange – indeed, just as their literary predecessors would have done, many years before.

Hold on, we're onto something here. When did this begin?

As the first to be conferred the status of a UNESCO-designated City of Literature in 2004, Edinburgh wears a unique, exclusive crown. There was a new flag to fly. By returning to those meetings-of-minds that fed ideas into the Scottish Enlightenment, and by carving relationships between writers, artists, publishers, educators, and industry specialists, the Edinburgh Literary Salon was reborn.

The Salon continued the Spirit of Enlightenment in The Wash Bar, which straddles the neatly ordered New Town and the rambling Old Town wynds. Who'd have thought a few ales or glasses of wine would find writers, poets, publishers, etc. discussing everything from Scottish feudalism to Roland Barthes? Robert Burns, probably. Not too long after new sensibilities (and the draining of the Nor' Loch) put a stop to dooking witches, Edinburgh became a crucible of thought, wisdom, and creativity – with a good dose of polemic tossed in.

Burns and his fellow Saloneers were around in revolutionary times... and so are we. Every century begins with new hope, albeit short-lived. Twentieth-century hope quickly diminished through war. That *fin de siècle* optimism as we approached the Millennium was high but false, full of media hype and expectation. Sure, there was no millennium bug, yet neither were those millennium goals achieved, even to Make Poverty History. The Literary

Salon, set up shortly after, also seemed destined not to survive.

Our capital city may be inspiring, but it doesn't always inspire capital, despite the natty pun in its Council's slogan. In the cut-throat world of commerce, anybody running a free event always fears the funding axe. And that's what happened to the Literary Salon, a little over ten years later, when the plug was pulled, and the City of Literature funds flowed away.

But writers are resilient and resourceful. They are also, by dint of their craft, solitary creatures, and for the die-hards of the Salon, the need to gather and blether proved imperative. When they heard 'The Salon is dead', they responded with 'Long live the Salon'.

Thus it was given yet another new beginning, born from the grassroots community of folk for whom the former Literary Salon was seen as a part of Edinburgh's palimpsestic history. A phoenix, rich in spark and fire, but impoverished: run by a voluntary Steering Group, on a budget of zero, through the kindness of guest speakers, the generosity of sponsors and donors, and a welcoming venue at The Wash Bar.

It was, nonetheless, a Renaissance.

Which begs another question: where did this book begin? That one is easier to answer. Put a bunch of writers together to run an event with no cash and a small amount of alcohol flowing, and at least one of them will come up with a plan that could cut this foreword down to four words: 'Let's publish an *anthology*!' As people who consider themselves 'thinkers', it would be ironic to call this a no-brainer.

Whether to raise money, engage with our community, or simply to have a body of work that said, 'Here we are, the reborn Edinburgh Literary Salon, sharing our passion for words and creative excellence', we knew, as soon as those four words were uttered, that this would happen. And where better to engage in the process than with one of our city's fine universities, which also runs an esteemed publishing course for postgraduates?

Off we travelled to Holy Corner, to Edinburgh Napier University, cap in hand (the same one we'd doffed to John Knox), with an embryonic idea and an obvious theme: Renaissance. Straight away, another new and fruitful relationship, based on previous practice, was born, and the Anthology Project was on the cards. We began to invite some of our associates to contribute and planned to put out a call for further submissions.

Then something unexpected happened: that millennium bug appeared twenty years late in the form of a global pandemic called COVID-19.

While the world was in lockdown, and the loneliness of the long-distance writer was made more acute, our theme of Renaissance became apposite. During lockdown, many of us felt lost. We were all, collectively, looking for a way out. It is hard to say whether we all found ways of getting through the anxiety that living through such virulent turbulence caused, but as writers, thinkers, creators, and makers, we had something to focus on.

After all, isn't the purpose of art to comfort the disturbed? Or to disturb the comfortable? Either way, this anthology has emerged from a city that has lived hand-in-hand with hardship and richness. This anthology is for everybody, just as the Literary Salon is open to all. During the pandemic, we explored ways to keep our community going online and connected with people from India to California, from the Highlands and far northern isles of our country to the southern reaches of the UK.

Edinburgh is a place of great diversity. Whether you come from the Stockbridge Colonies or the Banana Flats in Leith, the Old Town tenements or the southside suburbs, the words and ideas of this book will not lie still on the page, just as writers – albeit static and solitary creatures – are never stationary. Whether you are lost, still looking, or have found the answer, this book is for you.

When did the Literary Salon begin? Perhaps it was always thus. So here's a hand, my trusty fiere. According to Robert Louis Stevenson: 'We are all travellers in the wilderness of this world and the best we can find in our travels is an honest friend.'

Welcome to *Lost, Looking & Found*. We hope you find it an honest friend.

Lost

JAMES FLOWERDEW

The Man From '53

Mary Paulson-Ellis

The storm blows in like a guest that never should have crossed the door – unexpected, with a smile on its face, no warning of what is to come. One moment, the sea is flat, breeze dancing with the scent of the whins. The next, the light is gone, the sky a heavy threat. Out in the bay, the water begins with its churn.

In the playground, we stop jumping elastics to stare at the cauldron of the ocean, the gleam on its froth. A birl of wind lifts our hair; drops away. In the sudden stillness, even the birds are silent. Then we hear the teachers calling:

Come in, now. Come in.

'I'll take you to the Watts' house after school, Lara.'

It is Mrs Wiseman who makes the decision as the first angry raindrops sting the classroom windows. Outside, the slender birches submit to the wind. I know what it means: tonight, I will not be going home.

Mr and Mrs Watt used to live in Seatown, the old village hunkered between the cliff and the shore. But they stay up top now, like most, in bungalows built with money from the oil. I'd like to live up top, all my friends at the door. But Dad prefers the old houses, with their tiny windows and gable ends to the sea.

Mrs Wiseman drops me off at 4:45 p.m. The rain slashes at the car windscreen, wind whistling through the rubber seals.

'You'll be all right.'

It isn't really a question. I've stayed with the Watts a few times. The road up to the top is a hard one. Sometimes going down, too.

'That you, Lara?' Mrs Watt is in her kitchen, clattering the pans. 'Put your bag in the usual place.'

The spare room smells of camphor, a slight damp to the frill that trims the pillowcase. I dump my bag on the bed, go to the dressing table. The doll is still there.

In the living room, the coal-effect fire displays its steady whirr of red and black. Mr Watt stands at the window, hands in his pockets.

'That's it coming in, now,' he says.

I join him, hands in my pockets, too.

'Will it be a bad one?' I ask.

'Aye, no doubt.'

'Who's it coming for this time?'

'Not you, lassie. Not you.'

Last time there was a big storm, my father disappeared for three whole days, somewhere between Forties and Viking. There was a lot of praying then, everyone crowding in till Mum pushed them out. Then there was just me and her, and a cluster of dirty cups abandoned on the kitchen table.

Bloody God-botherers.

That was what she said. But all their prayers worked. Dad turned up halfway down the coast, orange of his jacket bright against the sea.

'We thought he was a goner.'

The man from the coastguard stood in the back porch with his boots still on, as he gave Mum the news. She stood at the sink, wrist-deep in dirty water.

'Not this time,' she said.

Dad came home. For a week. Then he went out again, returned in time for tea with a bucket full of mackerel, silver bellies and watery flanks. Mum's hands were shaking as she scaled the fish into the basin. His oilskins dripped onto the floor.

Mr Watt used to follow the fish when he was younger.

'There's the land,' he told me once. 'Then there's the boat, and the distance between them. Then there's the sea.'

A chasm of black.

That's what Mr Watt calls the ocean.

'Don't want to be spending your life searching that wilderness if you can help it.'

'Did you ever go overboard?' I asked.

We were standing at the living room window then, too, doll clutched in my hand. He smiled.

'No. But I brought one up once.'

'What, a mermaid?' My eyes widened. Mr Watt's glimmered.

'Don't be daft, lassie. A dead one. A fisherman gone to the beyond.'

A body, he meant, nose and ears nibbled.

'What was it like?'

'Bloated. Like a seal left too long in the sun.'

'Wattie.'

Mrs Watt's needles click-clacked from where she sat on the far side of the coal-effect fire. There was a warning in her voice.

'Who was it?' I held my breath, tight in my chest. Mr Watt rubbed at his ear.

'Jonah,' he said. Then he laughed.

After supper, Mr Watt sits in the front porch so he can watch the waves roll in. He likes the idea of the ocean tickling his toes. He belongs down in Seatown, at the edge, where he came from, not up here on the hill. The rain falls as though preparing for Noah, water washing the streets. I think of the river it will make of the path by our front door, that short run to the harbour. The sky is a streak of black; beneath it, the tide, rising. Just like in 1953.

At school, we've been learning about what happened in '53. The big storm. The tidal surge so huge it swept the path to the next village off the cliff, no way for them to escape but up the sharp incline of the brae behind the houses. So massive it took three homes from Seatown, nothing left but their back gables and a bathtub hanging out. I laughed at that the first time Mr Watt told me.

'What's funny?' he said.

'That the sea left behind a bathtub.'

He pulled at his earlobe. 'Aye. Right enough.'

The storm in '53 went on for three days. Just like the one that took my dad. Waves higher than a man. Waves higher than a house. Waves higher than anything anyone had seen before.

'Higher than a giant?' I asked.

'Probably.' Mr Watt sucked on the e-cig Mrs Watt had given him to save his lungs. 'No one could go out, nothing to do but sit and wait, see what was left after.'

Like we are doing, now. Together we watch the ocean rise towards us.

'Tell me again about the man from '53 who was washed away and came back,' I say. 'Like Jonah.'

'Jonah weren't washed,' says Mr Watt. 'He were swallowed.'

'Swallowed then. Swallowed by the sea.'

Mr Watt doesn't reply. Vapour trickles from his nostrils.

'It couldn't really have been three days he disappeared for, could it?' I say.

'Who knows?' Mr Watt grunts. 'Who knows how long once the sea's got you?'

'He wasn't even in the water.' Mrs Watt appears behind us with a mug of tea. 'Went up the brae like everyone else.'

Mr Watt twists in his chair. 'Why did no one see him for three days then?'

'Had the bottle with him, didn't he?' Her lips twitch. 'No way he'd leave that behind.'

In '53, the sea took everything. The sheds at midpoint. The garages by the harbour. The gasworks in Banff. The roof of the Breadalbane cinema got blown to kingdom come, that's what the old folk say.

'What did the man do after?' I ask. 'When they found him.'

Mr Watt draws on his e-cig. 'He just got on with it, I reckon.'

'With what?'

'Living.'

But what is living after you've been dead, or at least inside the whale? That's what I'm thinking. Who are you then?

That evening, I fit the plug to the Watt's bathtub, let the water run in. It has a green quality to it, like the water in the bay when the sun beats down. I step inside – one leg, two legs – hold my breath, skin a sudden blaze. Then I crouch down.

The doll floats on the surface, a lazy turn in the water. Like she would float if she was with my father, I think, hair fanning out as they surf the waves. Along the edge of the bath are all the things I've brought with me, just in case. A pebble with a hole in it. A dried fish-egg sac. Half a sea-urchin. A piece of glass, green like the bathwater. I lie back, hold the glass to my eye, think of the man from '53 staring through a tiny window in the gable end, salt splatter all over the pane. What did he think when the sea came for him? Did he open the door?

'You all right in there, Lara?'

Mrs Watt is outside on the landing. She'll be fetching one of her old nightgowns for me, ribbon threaded through the neck, faint stink of mothballs. I rest my toe on the chill of the cold tap. It's been two days since my dad went out in his boat. One day since the storm stole in. Sixty-four days since New Year.

My mum disappeared for three days once, didn't even leave a note. Everyone thought she'd gone in the water, too. The God-botherers ran down to the shore and along the beach, as though they might catch her. The pebbles wouldn't let up with their rattle.

Turns out she'd flit to Edinburgh.

'Another black chasm.'

That was what Mr Watt whispered when he found out. She didn't return until the new year had been and gone, and then only to pack a bag.

'She always was a bugger, your mum.'

That was what Mrs Watt said when I told her, gave me a sort of sideways hug. Mrs Watt's jumpers smell of mothballs, too.

I lift the doll from the bathwater, stare at it. Drowning, the replacement of one thing for another – air for water, water for air. Then I pull the doll's head from its body. When the bathwater runs out, all that's left is a tumble of body parts gathered in the drain.

That night, I dream of being inside the whale. Me with the doll in my fist. Mum with her hair like the doll's. Dad is the furthest away, standing in the whale's throat, orange jacket bright, waiting for his moment. I don't have time to wave.

In the morning, I wake, and it's as though the storm never existed. Mrs Watt sets an egg down for me, some soft white bread to mop up the yolk. We eat in silence, nothing but the cat scratching at the back door. Mr Watt drinks the last of his tea, pats my hand.

'Come on now and we'll watch for a moment before you have to go.'

'Dishes,' says Mrs Watt.

Mr Watt flaps an arm. 'Aye, woman. Later.'

Together we stand at the living room window, looking through the glass at an ocean that's flat to the horizon.

'That's it over then,' Mr Watt says.

'Till next time,' I reply.

I go to school. The scent of coconut from the gorse falls from the hill. In the classroom I gaze out at the slender birches stretching upwards, imagine the man from '53 coming down the brae.

'Lara.' The teacher summons me. 'Turn to the front.'

I do what I'm told. But inside, I am praying:

When I get home, my father's boots will be abandoned in the porch,
His oilskins will be dripping.
My mother will be standing with her hands in the water,
Mackerel bellies flashing silver.

I will open the door, and they will turn to me: one, then the other.

'Did you miss me?' I'll say.

When I get home.

Mary Paulson-Ellis writes detective stories about those who die with no next of kin. She is the author of three novels set in Edinburgh, the home of the Literary Salon: *The Other Mrs Walker* (a *Times* Bestseller and Waterstones Scottish Book of the Year 2017); *The Inheritance of Solomon Farthing* (long-listed for the McIlvanney Prize for Scottish Crime Book of the Year 2020); and *Emily Noble's Disgrace*. When not wandering in graveyards, Mary likes to write about the murderous side of family life.

The Apple

Sara Sheridan

Eve shouldn't have shared.
Sisters!
The world would belong to us
if only she'd held back
so many delicious secrets,
like babes in our bellies.

Instead: given freely.
We are bitten.
Snake stung.

Pained.
And there was no need.
For Eve could have eaten
Every.
Single.
Bite.

Sara Sheridan has written more than twenty books and works in both commercial fiction and non-fiction, several of which have made the bestsellers charts. Her work has been shortlisted for the Wilbur Smith, Saltire, and David Hume prizes. She is fascinated by history and its impact on our lives, researching not only in archives but using historical artefacts, art, and the fabric of our built and rural environment. Sara has been a sporadic attendee of the Literary Salon for over a decade. She loves being by the sea, is a voracious reader, and is a campaigner for equality issues (currently supporting the Witches of Scotland campaign).

Now, Then

Sharon Sampson

NOW

I am a fully-grown adult, but you started me, brought me into this world. Every fold of my brain, the fingers I use to write this sentence and the eyes that read what I type on the screen were formed within your very being.

Your blood once filled my veins, your heart beat life into mine, and four decades on it's still going strong. What an extraordinary thing, to create a whole new person with your own body and push them out into the world.

Your DNA, and that of my (absent) father's, mapped out the territory I call 'myself'. I am the product of thousands of years of ancestry; of gene pools mixing, merging, muddying the waters. My red hair, the result of a timely match with a recessive gene on your side and my father's genetic code.

Now, mere remnants of that primal, life-giving bond exist between us. The strong, thick cords of placenta and fibrous tissue which bound us together are but a memory. Gradually, the unseen rope which connects us unravelled down to a few remaining strands.

At first glance, they appear fragile, frayed as they are by long-forgotten resentments, anger spoken in pain, words which tore apart the very breath between us.

But they endure.

THEN

I was very much a wanted baby. You loved my dad.

The love of your life, you always told me. Your romance spanned three years, filled with laughter and holidays away together. It ended when you became pregnant with me.

A tearful, wrenching break-up which left you a young single mother in the '70s. For a girl from a 'good' family, this was beyond shameful in the eyes of neighbours, family friends, and wider society.

Of course, the shame was on you, not the reckless, immature, selfish young man who was jointly responsible.

You loved me anyway. We were happy anyway.

Photos of us then show you looking slim, young and elegant. Your dark shiny hair is cut into the fashionable pageboy style of the time.

Me, a chubby-faced ginger baby, in blue corduroy dungarees, Superman pyjamas, and fluffy Orville the Duck slippers.

My favourite picture is the photo of four generations. I can't be more than two months old, lying contentedly in the arms of my great-grandmother, with you standing at the side of the wing-back chair next to Gran.

What strikes a chord in my heart is the pride evident in each of your faces.

My early childhood was a Blyton-flavoured bliss. I never wanted for love, time, or affection.

You played guitar and sang to me, your soft, melodic voice skimming gently over my favourite songs.

Whenever I hear that song, 'The Lord of the Dance', I am transported back in time. We sang the chorus together:

'Dance, then, wherever you may be
I am the Lord of the dance,' said He,
'And I'll lead you all wherever you may be,
And I'll lead you all in the dance,' said He.'

We had a second-hand upright piano in the living-room. It was placed against the wall at the far end of the room.

You sat down at the piano most days, and I played with my picture blocks or colouring books as the room filled with Beethoven sonatas and Bach studies.

Sometimes I got to sit on the piano stool with you and press the chunky, slidey keys with my toddler fingers.

To me, the piano was a giant musical toy, its workings a mystery to my child's mind. I thought that when you played, you performed some sort of magic.

So, imagine my joy when I got a piano of my own one Christmas! It was a miniature grand, made of shiny, solid black plastic, with keys just the right size for my tiny hands. When you sat down to play, I arranged my piano next to yours and plonked out my own compositions.

NOW
When I imagine being a mother myself, I plan to teach my son or daughter how to play. I vow that there will always be a piano in the house.

Musical talent runs like a golden thread throughout our family. My great-grandfather taught my gran, who taught you, and you both taught me.

I want to pass down that love of music to my child and give them every opportunity to learn any instrument they want, whether it's piano and violin like me, or the tuba or drums!

My love of music has enriched my life and it's not about being the next great musician or prodigy, but simply appreciating the joy of being able to play.

THEN

From my upbringing I will cherry-pick the best parts and pass them down.

The love of books, which you instilled in me from a young age (I was one of the few kids in the class who could read before starting school).

An appreciation of all genres of music from classical, to rock, and even country. You taught me to have the patience to sit with a problem until I found a solution. Whether it was a jigsaw puzzle or maths homework, you made me believe in my ability to tackle anything.

When I was growing up, you were by necessity a strong, independent woman. To this day I admire those qualities in you, and I have tried hard to strengthen those traits in myself.

From you I learned how to decorate. Remember the horror of trying to hang matching wallpaper in the kitchen in our old house?

You taught me to put up shelves and curtain poles and fix temperamental central heating boilers, to unblock a sink and wire a plug.

They say that 'necessity is the mother of invention', and in our house, a knife served as a screwdriver, a high heel became a hammer to hang pictures on the wall, and we measured things with our hands and feet when the measuring tape went missing.

THEN

My ex-partner and I sit in the pink leather chairs in the consultant's room. Apparently, he is the fertility doctor. He answers my ex-partner's question. I am listening but I don't understand.

He carries on writing with one of those faux fountain pens, scratching out black ink in a column in my notes.

'Sorry, Doctor, did you say *two per cent*?' I ask.

He signs his initials at the end of his entry, flicks his pen to the side, and looks up.

'Yes. Two per cent at the very most.' He leans back in his chair and levels his gaze at mine. 'Given your age and other reproductive factors, my professional opinion rests there.'

He continues talking to my ex-partner. I hear her thank him. I stand up when she does, I shake the doctor's hand and walk in slow motion out of the room.

I realise later that the doctor was trying to be kind when he gave us that two percent. It was a kick in the guts, but better than a zero.

So, I will never be a biological mother.

I will not nurture a tiny human in the depths of my belly.

I will never know what it's like to feel my baby kick, to see them grow at each scan, or hear their heartbeat.

There will be no daughter to pass on my love of

books or music to, no school plays to attend as a proud, beaming parent because my child is a tree in the forest background.

No teenager to argue with or guide through adolescence and their experience of first love.

No university graduation where I drink too much Prosecco and embarrass them with my loud, gushing pride.

There will be none of these things.

But I tell myself that there will be other things.

Life is a perpetual cycle of death and rebirth.

Now, I will mourn my loss. I will cry and grieve for as long as my heart aches.

But then, I will prepare for a rebirth.

For life must go on.

NOW

'Do you have P.E. today? Where's your lunch bag?' I ask as I frantically try to brush her hair before she leaves for school.

A nod of the head means 'yes' for P.E., as my partner appears from the living room holding the lunch bag in question.

'Right kiddo, trainers on and we're good to go,' I say as she puts her hairband in place and moves to grab her shoes from the hall.

Ready at last, we all head to the car for the morning school run. I race her to try and be first into the car, but she always has her seatbelt on before me.

'I won. Again!' she shouts from the back, victorious.

An ordinary exchange between parents and kids up and down the country on a school morning, but what seems ordinary and mundane on the outside feels extraordinary to me.

When I first met my partner, he was slightly worried that having a daughter would put me off, but of course it didn't.

He is very much a hands-on dad who is involved in every aspect of his daughter's life, so from the beginning I knew that he was a package deal.

When we became serious, we knew it was time for me to meet his daughter. Was I nervous? Scared? Absolutely! But I was also excited to meet the little person who means the world to him.

Meeting her for the first time was more nerve-racking than when I first met my partner. I respect children and I understand that their trust and respect must be earned. I couldn't assume that just because I'm generally good with kids, she would instantly like me.

So much rested on us getting along, but after about fifteen minutes in her company, I knew I had nothing to worry about.

We were soon chatting and laughing, and over time, our bond has become stronger and stronger.

She is such a precious kid, and while I am by no means a parental figure, I am a big part of her life, which means the world to me.

A few years have passed since that day in the consultant's office, but it feels more like a lifetime. Life does indeed go on, in ways I had not dared to imagine.

Sharon Sampson has published various short stories and essays over the last few years. Her fiction usually has a dystopian or Gothic theme, while her essays are inspired by her political views or personal experience. She holds a Creative Writing MA and she is writing her first non-fiction book which she hopes to have completed by the end of this year. Sharon has been a member of the Literary Salon for two years and says the camaraderie of the group has been a real inspiration.

Renaissance

Sadie Maskery

They have freed us from quiet.
They thought it would lead to rebirth,
that place of (stillness), learning
to live with only ourselves,
see things grow when given
          hope. A new life/new choices
when the cocoon / s p l i t /
that was the plan.
Stillborn. (Gone to s h i t.)
I want to celebrate, I try.
They have released us
back to busy-ness,
consumption for the greater good.
Life is hum and buzz and bright lights,
grunting laughter, the frightening kind –
at, not with (packs hunting).
Bottled up then / s m a s h /
all that energy bursts, spatters,
              smears streets
        with trash, catcalls,
piss on walls.

Pubs closed – attention falls
to green places.
What did they expect?
A new world of kind faces?
They thought the change would
bring an age of *utopian joy*.
They just showed us new things
to d e s t r o y.

Sadie Maskery has poetry in anthologies by various publishers including British Fantasy Society, Green Ink, and Narala Press. She has lived near nature and the sea for many years, and it often influences her poetry. This is Sadie's first collaboration with the Literary Salon and Merchiston Publishing but hopefully not her last.

Even When You're No Longer Around You Will Hear Me

Regi Claire

The end-of-tether feeling started a fortnight ago, after Mrs Rivers' clothes airer collapsed and her toaster caught fire. A few days later her juicer malfunctioned, giving off sparks.

'If they're faulty products, take them back to the shop, Mum, or return them to the makers. Happens all the time with this cheap shit,' her son said when he visited.

Faulty product — return to maker. The words have stayed in Mrs Rivers' mind, slowly corroding her.

Ever since her illness several years earlier, her body has been misbehaving. Sometimes her legs buckle or her heart goes into overdrive. And on this fine June morning, washing up her breakfast things, she suddenly feels hot all over, steaming almost. Just the soapy water, she tells herself, ignore it. Beyond the honeysuckle that has begun to overgrow the kitchen window, the Smiths' tabby patrols the sunny back wall between the properties. The crows caw, then caw again; dew glistens on the leaves of the oak tree where the birds have gathered to monitor her activities; and the night's cool breaths withdraw into the darkness under the bushes to wait out the day.

'Faulty product – return to maker,' she whispers. After two weeks of corrosion, two weeks of various attempts to redeem herself – and as many failures – she has finally, and with considerable endurance, come to the end of her tether. Everyone, Mrs Rivers believes, has a certain length allotted to them. Some tethers never exceed umbilical cords. Some furl out into the open, through gardens and streets, before getting trampled into the dirt. But a few grow thicker, stronger with every year, twining themselves round others to reach even further, until they span the whole world – which, once in their power, they truss up like a trundling turkey ready for the carve-up.

She shakes her head. Her husband would have told her not to be fanciful, to get a grip and get on with the dishes. She seizes the tea towel. Her husband isn't here anymore; *his* tether was rather shorter than average. She flicks the towel, then flicks it again, harder. She should be glad to still be alive. *Count your blessings*, everyone says. *Thank your lucky stars*. Well, dammit, she'd have been happy to kick the bucket, kick the bucket and be done with it. Forty-six wouldn't have been such a bad innings.

Gris-Gris, the crow with white wing markings, is on the lawn now, stabbing its beak into the grass at random while swivelling sharp glances at her and at the cat.

Mrs Rivers picks up the bowl of cold porridge, unlocks the back door. At the creak of the hinges the other crows fly down from the tree and come hopping towards her, sleek-feathered and plump. She slops out the leftovers, then stands for a moment as the birds squabble over the grainy grey lumps. She is about to go back inside when a flash of light makes her look over at the Smiths' house. Framed behind an upstairs window is curly-haired Lulubelle, their youngest. Are those binoculars she is holding?

Mrs Rivers gives a wave and the girl waves back quite naturally it seems, with both hands. For an instant she sees herself as the child would, a hesitant figure bent like a question mark. Instead of returning indoors as she intended, she steps over to the honeysuckle, towards the clenched purple flowers that have always reminded her of cats' claws dripping blood. She snaps off several stems. She'll put them in a vase; who knows, they might outlive her. The Smiths' tabby, meanwhile, has stretched out on the wall, taking the sun in disdain.

Faulty product — return to maker / Faulty product — return to maker beats a harsh rhythm through Mrs Rivers' body as she crosses and recrosses her kitchen, tidying up. Yes, she thinks, that's me all right: I am the faulty product. All my life I've been faulty. Not enough flesh where it matters, too much in the wrong places, straight hair when it should have been curly like Lulubelle's. A curved spine, crooked teeth. Then the cancer. Count your blessings, she tells herself, you've survived. And before she can stop herself, she spits on the floor.

The previous week, after her return-to-maker query at the post office, Mrs Rivers spat on the pavement, quite deliberately.

'What? What is it you want?' the postmaster had asked. 'If you wish to send a parcel, nothing beyond thirty kilos goes into the van. If it's livestock, you'll need a licence. Health and Safety. But you of all people ought to know. Wasn't your husband employed by the Council?

The Council can advise further. Unless you wish to apply for a passport?' And with a 'Next please!' he handed her a form.

So Mrs Rivers contacted the Council. All she desired, she explained carefully, was to be posted back to her maker, whoever that was. Surely the government, almighty and foresightful, would have a way of offering this service to its citizens, or was it 'clients' these days? The woman at the end of the line, probably with impatient blue-lacquered fingernails, said again, 'But which service, madam? Recycling? Would that be it? For large items you can phone special uplift or go directly to one of the household waste recycling centres. If it's a passport application, you'll need to visit the post office. We don't....'

The church didn't offer much consolation either. They told Mrs Rivers she would require faith and decorum. Lots of it. Enough to fill the nave at least. Which made her smile. Religion hadn't changed much, it seemed.

So here she is now, seated at her kitchen table with a cup of milky rooibos. She gazes at the sprays of honeysuckle trailing from the vase in the centre of the table. What next? There's all this talk about moving heaven and earth, but she has tried both and found them wanting. Only one thing left – she recalls her earlier sensation of sudden fierce heat, recalls the sparking juicer, the toaster filling the kitchen with smoke... No doubt a solution will present itself; possibly some special particle accelerator to expedite matters?

When the doorbell rings, Mrs Rivers doesn't glance up. Let them ring, ring, and bloody ring until doomsday or at least until the wires short.

The ringing stops. One of the crows croaks angrily, then the windowpane pings as it so often does when an insect misjudges the distance between the honeysuckle and the glass. Poor thing must have brained itself. A sudden flurry of pings makes her look over in time to see a small hand disappear below the sill. What the...? Mrs Rivers feels a moment's dizziness as she stands up. Then she flings open the back door and here is Lulubelle, the tabby beside her.

'Oh,' the child says, dropping a fistful of sand. 'Hello, Mrs Rivers.'

'Lulubelle?' Mrs Rivers says.

The girl hangs her head and retreats a few steps. 'I didn't break your window, did I? I knew you were home; I saw you feed the crows earlier. And last night when I couldn't sleep I saw you feed the hedgehog. And the night before I saw you—'

'Yes, yes,' interrupts Mrs Rivers. Perhaps it's the curly hair that annoys her, golden almost and glossy as corn silk in the sun. 'Have you been spying on me?'

Lulubelle skips away and picks something up. 'These are for you.' She holds out a paper plate with three pink-glazed fairy cakes. They have painted-on blue eyes and smiling rosebud mouths.

Mrs Rivers reaches out, then looks from the cakes to Lulubelle. Her eyes fasten on the girl's face; there's a red rash all over the cheeks. Hurriedly she says, 'Did you make them yourself?'

The child nods and Mrs Rivers' grip on the plate loosens, making the cakes slide. 'How very kind. But you really ought to be in bed, Lulubelle. Where are your parents? I think you might have the measles. Or maybe scarlet fever.'

As she tries to inch the door closed, the tabby shoots past her, leaps on the table and starts lapping up the tea.

'Shoo,' Mrs Rivers says, turning towards the animal. She dumps the plate on the worktop and flaps her hands. 'Shoo. Be off with you!'

The cat hisses and now Lulubelle, who has followed him inside, speaks up: 'Toby here knows you want rid of me, and he doesn't like it. Neither do I. I'm not as stupid as you think. You're old and sad. That's why you feed all those wild animals. But why not care for your neighbours for a change? I brought you these cakes. Let's eat them.' The child keeps tagging after her round the table until Mrs Rivers feels so dizzy she has to sit down.

'That's better,' Lulubelle says, settling on the chair opposite.

The child is behaving like an adult, it occurs to Mrs Rivers. And those eyes are far too—

Lulubelle giggles, wipes at her horrible red spots and they crumble and fall off. She licks her fingers. 'It's sugar, silly Mrs Rivers. Bits of icing sugar!'

The cat jumps to the floor. There are scrunching noises; for a moment he stares up at Mrs Rivers, his teeth stained crimson, and she sees herself emblazoned in his eyes.

Her dizziness grows worse.

Now the girl pulls out a smartphone, holds it up. 'Smile, please.'

Mrs Rivers shrinks away. The last thing she wants is to have her photo taken, and certainly not by this child or whatever she is.

'Caught you,' Lulubelle says. 'Now you'll stay inside my camera. You see, I talk to my pictures. And I shall talk to you tonight when I can't sleep. You will hear my voice in the dark. Even when you're no longer around you will hear me.' Again she giggles and begins to dance away, scooping up the tabby.

The back door is shut when Mrs Rivers comes to, slumped at the kitchen table, a half-cup of cold rooibos beside her. She blinks. There is no sign of the plate with the fairy cakes, only a sprinkle of red crumbs on the floor. So that's it, she thinks, that's how things will be from now on. No particle accelerator, nothing to expedite matters. Just the odd crumb here and there. And a little girl's threats to keep you on your toes.

Mrs Rivers pushes herself upright, then goes to fetch her mail – the usual newspaper, also several circulars she throws straight into the bin, forget the recycling. She scans the paper's headlines: 'Elephants without tusks – evolutionary ploy to avoid extinction?', 'Eternal life thanks to technology?'

After a fresh cup of tea she feels more or less restored to her own faulty self. She is about to get on with her housework when she notices the honeysuckle in the vase. The stems seem to have become longer, more sinewy, ready to strangle anything in their path; and the flowers are all open now, their stamens undulating luxuriously, as though tasting the air.

Lulubelle lowers her binoculars and Toby shifts in her lap, purring. Mrs Rivers has just stepped out of her back door. She is wearing bright yellow gloves – washing-up gloves? – and carrying the vase from the table, also what looks like a carving knife. Lulubelle smirks as she watches her neighbour hurl the vase against the house wall, stamp on the spilled greenery, then set upon the honeysuckle beside the kitchen window, slashing and slashing.

By the time Mrs Rivers has finished, the ground is covered with a tumble of twigs, and the shrub barely reaches her knees – but it is alive, and Lulubelle knows that's what counts. She nods to herself, murmurs, 'So, Mrs Rivers, you really think this is how it ends?' From the paper plate next to her she picks up the last of the fairy cakes. Weighing it in her palm, she gazes at it for an instant, then with a snap she breaks the smiley face in two. One half she puts back on the plate, the other she eats, chewing slowly, deliberately, first the single blue eye, next the cheek, finally the ruined rosebud mouth. Toby has stopped purring. A claw grazes Lulubelle's arm as if by accident, and she lets him lick the sugar glaze off her fingers. Then, stroking him with one hand, she brings out her phone, begins to scroll through her photo gallery.

Over the years the gallery will grow and grow. Until it contains people of all ages, shapes, races, creeds – all of them clamouring to be released into a new, better world.

Regi Claire was shortlisted for the Forward Prizes 2020 and won the Mslexia/PBS Women's Poetry Competition 2019. She is the winner of a UBS Cultural Foundation award and a two-time finalist for the Saltire Scottish Book of the Year awards. Regi enjoys going to the Salon for the literary chit-chat and the chance to catch up with old friends over a glass of wine. You might observe her talking to her retriever in a mishmash of Swiss German and English as they walk the streets, escorted by a gang of crows and magpies demanding kibble.

Unless Life

Jim Mackintosh

i

We travelled the roads of our lives alone
in our extended herds

ii

Now	as then
we are the pickaxe	to the mournful earth
We are the needle	in the global bloodstream
of the desperate	We are the reconstruct
from hell	We are the oppressed
breaths that br	oke the journey, the rebirth
of our	humanity

iii

The sky	holds a mirror
to the mouth	of what we've
become	A pale
shadow	is in our head
For now we	need go
not a death	further

iv

Ask why	the wealthy soared
interwoven with	the poor settling
into the traps	of normals
to challenge	everything, to live
to survive	only to die again
without hope	in another life

v

Another layer of	ash
settles	on the bed
of the Rubicon	Hand in pocket
I take comfort	still
in the fabric	of a mask

vi

It is not enough anymore just to be unless life happens

Jim Mackintosh is the Makar of the Federation of Writers Scotland. He is therefore either writing, editing, or thinking about writing or editing poetry every day. He is never more happy than when stravaigin' the hills, glens, and woods of his native Perthshire. Although not shy at hugging a tree or gossiping wi' a squirrel, he fair misses hugging and hae'in a news wi' pals and the random joy of Literary Salon events, real-life Book Festivals, and most importantly, drams afterwards in Sandy Bell's.

Incubation

Devana Senanayake

'Thank you so much, dear,' she said as I handed the breakfast to her.

I smiled and left her to eat in peace. I met her again, later in the day, as I shuffled into her room to collect the breakfast tray and place her lunch on her desk. She seemed tired but continued to smile and nod at me, the skin around her eyes creased.

When I pushed the cart through the empty corridors to hand over her dinner, family members stood outside her door in tears.

'Oh, it happens all the time here,' my supervisor, Deb, told me on my first day. Her eyes mimicked a practiced concern and care. 'It takes some time, but you get used to it.'

I never did.

In the summer of 2017, I had a job as a food attendant in a private hospital.

My day started the same. Every morning, I got up at five. I made the bed, brushed my teeth, and put on my uniform. I liked my clothes pressed to perfection – smooth and creaseless.

With an extra dash of cinnamon, I boiled coffee in a pan until it burned a bit. For breakfast, I had a piece of blackened toast, salted butter, and homemade sauerkraut.

I ran to the train station for a 6:30 a.m. start. When the train arrived, the sky hovered over me like a thick, black cloak. When I arrived at the hospital, rays of light seeped through the clouds.

Before I entered the kitchen, I used a fishnet cap to cover my hair. Several people ran in and out. I entered chaos: the hiss of pans, the bubble of pots, the slice of knives, the click of freezer doors, and the cacophony of voices. I remember the omnipresence of steam.

Deb stood over everyone. She had a spoon in her hand. She raised it to command attention. And tapped it on the doors to demand order.

Several mediocre young men were spotlighted as her 'favourites'. When she spoke to them she smiled; her irises expanded and she leaned in closer to listen to them.

When I tried to talk to her, she raised her nose and surveyed me in deep suspicion.

'Hello, you,' she said and forced a smile. 'On time, yes?'

'Hi Deb. I need that key for the door. Do you have it? I told you at the end of last month,' I said.

'Oh, did you? There are no spare keys today. Take this,' she said and handed me a tablespoon. 'Knock it on the doors if you have trouble entering.'

I rolled my eyes at her.

'Chop, chop, onto your shift,' she chimed. She clapped the large spoon in her palm to add a flamenco-like flair to the gesture. Today, she had on a bold red lip.

Deb had been a natural beauty in her youth; I could see it in the shape of her face. She had relied on it to control and command but her dependence on it had not translated into old age.

The hospital had thirty floors. Each floor, structured like a box, had twenty rooms and three steel elevators. I started in one room and moved through the box-shaped floor.

A series of bright ceiling lights led the path. Sometimes, the hospital had musicians play obscure instruments like ukuleles or harps.

When Peter – a poltergeist-like presence who roamed around Floor 10 – encountered this, he burbled cynically.

Each day I did the same thing. I collected meals from the kitchen. I distributed them across various floors allocated to me. I collected the finished trays once the meal had been consumed. I dropped the trays and any spare trash in the kitchen. Then I started the cycle all over again.

Each cycle took half an hour. I repeated each cycle sixteen times through an eight-hour shift.

I collected shifts for the hospital from a purple-coloured app. I had to constantly look at my phone to catch any available slots.

This set-up exacerbated my anxiety and everything felt elusive.

On Sundays I prepped meals. At Victoria Market I looked for the perfect cabbage. With it cupped in my arm like a baby, I rode the tram back home.

I cut it open, tenderly.

The first crackle felt like a breath. I could hear the release as I split the cabbage in half. The perfect exhale.

Once I sliced the entirety into thin threads, I carried it into a metal basin and sprinkled salt over it.

I then crunched the threads until the juice spilled out like fresh tears. I liked this. I liked that it felt mechanical and had the expected response. When insomnia hit me in the night, I sterilised glass jars in my oven. I stored dozens of these in my kitchen.

I used my palms to push each thread into place. I used my knuckles to pack it in. Next, I topped the jars full of the cabbage juice. The top had to be covered in juice or the batch could spoil.

When the odd leaf spoiled, the entire batch had to be discarded. I hated this. Fermentation took time.

Then I closed the jar and pushed the lock in. I never had to do much. As long as I stuck to the process, the rest fell into place.

'Darling, can you please help me get up?' she said as I held her hand. 'When you get older, I hope people are as nice to you as you are to me.'

I liked the old ladies. They opened up. They told me about themselves, their lives and mostly about the people they loved.

Then they died. They reminded me of silk that slipped through one's hand: lithe but memorable.

The old men, like Peter, never smiled.

One day, he asked me for peppermint tea.

'Love, can you please run and fetch me some honey too?' he mumbled, his nose buried deep in *The Age*.

When I brought the honey up, he suddenly remembered that he needed a dash of milk.

When I brought milk to his room, he had fallen asleep.

I placed it on his desk and closed the door. His snores resonated through the corridor.

'Hello. You have reached *Squid Hospitality Services*. This is Emma speaking. How may I help you?' a polite voice on the phone asked.

I mentioned my full name, candidate number, and the hospital they had stationed me at.

'I'd really like any available shifts, even if they are last minute,' I pressed. My voice had a tone of desperation – the kind that people never respond to.

'Oh, it's you,' Emma said in a saccharine voice that clearly implied I had been a topic of discussion.

She sounded simultaneously bored and annoyed. I pictured her on her desk. Feet up on the table. I could see Facebook open on her computer. While she scrolled through Instagram, she responded to calls.

'Any upcoming shifts should be available on the app. Please keep an eye on that. Bye!' she screeched.

I could never evoke pity in Emma.

A lot had happened.

My friends could smell my consistent dejection. My emotional capacity for philosophical conversations, brunch, beach days, and hikes disappeared. I had no interest in movies, lacklustre theatre, or overpriced music festivals.

My body could not mimic their liveliness anymore. Or appear to understand their problems. Or break into a forced smile.

My love for life curdled. I fantasised about consistency and routine and structure. But everything felt elusive. When previously I had been an active participant in life, I was now reduced to a passive and tired observer.

I met Minh at the hospital.

Minh had a thin frame but could single-handedly carry tables and doors. She had a clean face – no make-up. Her thin hair had been combed into a bun on her neck. Circular glasses framed her heart shaped face.

She asked me for my name the first day and filled me in on the details about her floor.

'Hey. So Rooms 10A-10J have received their breakfast. Can you check back in half an hour to collect their trays?' she said curtly. 'Thank you.'

It took her time to open up. When she saved dessert for me from the kitchen, I realised that she had decided we were friends.

Over lunch, she told me about her life. Minh studied medicine and hoped to be a nurse like her mother. With her mother and brother, she had immigrated to Australia in the late nineties. They had a hard life in Vietnam but had succeeded because of her mother's job as a nurse in Melbourne.

'Don't you feel tired at the end of the day?' I asked her.

'Yeah, but I need to save for a house. It's good to start early,' she said in her level-headed tone.

I only planned for my month's rent. I never even contemplated the thought of a house. Unlike all my uni friends, Minh had a good head on her shoulders. She had plans and laid the foundation for them but also looked out and checked up on the people around her. Though our encounters lasted only a couple of minutes, I could rely on her to guide me in the right direction.

'What do you do for your sore feet?' I complained.

'We all have that. Rest. Stretch a lot,' she said. 'I've got to get back. Talk soon?'

No one had a salve, even for my sore feet.

I had bills to pay; but the app did not signpost any available shifts.

'Hi Emma. I have checked my app multiple times and I have not received any slots. Is there a reason for this?' I asked her.

'Can you please continue to keep an eye on the app?' she said and slammed the phone.

I could feel her disconnect.

I suppose her emotional void appeared professional.

I could not sleep at night. I missed him – I missed us. I thought about him constantly.

I needed someone – anyone. I hated loneliness. But, at the same time, he had drained me of emotion and desire. I did not feel much.

I looked through various apps on my phone. I never started a conversation; I just liked to scroll through the multitude of options.

Who should I choose to be consumed by?

My lack of purpose and loneliness melted in the heated outpour of infatuation. It injected an illusion – a false purpose – a much needed distraction.

Well-travelled. I had no intention of listening to another sojourn through Europe. *Loves pets.* Too hands-on. Why are all his photos of his 'ripped' body? Is this meant to be a turn-on? Why is he smiling so much? I should ask him for his dentist's number. He has great teeth.

When apps bored me, I looked through listicles on the

internet. I had more or less tried everything they detailed but there was no improvement in my life.

I had nailed the art of the early morning; I tried celery juice; I tried to make art; I journaled; I exercised; I *#namaslayed* every other day; and I meditated multiple times.

Self-care and *self-love* could not replace the intimacy and care of another person. At this point of night, I had no need for pretence. I just needed a lover and their body. I did not need to build a metaphorical altar to 'me'.

I tried the next best option: I smoked and stared at the ceiling.

I hated that this perpetual loneliness had become my reality.

We had started the day at the museum. It had been a perfect summer day. A coolness pricked our skin.

They had a John Olsen exhibition. I remember the reddish backdrop and the incisive black dots. He had a faded maroon shirt – I liked the look of it. When he looked at the pictures, he leaned in to look at the details and then moved back to look at the overall picture. He repeated this movement until his curiosity had been satiated.

We then sat by the river and looked at the ducks. He picked up a branch to poke me. I had ripped the leaves, crunched it up and hurled it at his face.

When he picked up a book and dissolved into it, I looked at the sky....

With no sense of sleep and a deep intention to *move on*... I turned on Netflix and started to binge through the next episode of *Queer Eye*. The light from the screen burned into my eye.

'Where are you from? India? Jamaica?' he asked me as I pushed the trolley into the elevator. I had seen him run around the kitchen – I had never bothered to ask him his name.

'Neither of those places,' I said as I pressed the button of the next floor.

'I just can't figure you out. What are you?' he asked me. I did not understand his intention to make small talk.

'I am not a "what",' I told him as I rolled the trolley out of the elevator.

He never bothered me again.

'Are you another food attendant here? I have all these trays, can I give them to you?' I asked a prematurely balding man.

His eyes expanded and he looked closely at me.

'I'm a doctor here,' he said and extended his hand to the door. 'Please, take them in. When the door closes shut, it does not open again. Use the key they gave you… ' he mumbled as the door shut.

A cool draught slipped through. The corridor had dimmed lights and felt like a dark street. Fermentation stained every room – I could smell the bodies in decay.

The patients in this section had patches on their heads. Liver spots stained their skin. I could hear their disjointed exhales and their constant convulsions.

When I entered a room to collect the tray, I noticed the patient deep in sleep. He had not touched his food. I collected the tray and set it into the trolley. This action made a loud *clack*.

I looked behind me, he opened his eyes.

He stared at me…. He did not blink.

'Sorry,' I mumbled and pushed the trolley out of the room.

He sat up. And then sprang up like a jack-in-the-box. This startled me.

Why did he get up so suddenly?

When I left the room, I moved to the other end of the trolley to pull it. The trolley acted as a barrier that separated us. I looked around for a doctor, a nurse, or an attendant... anyone.

I could feel the intensity of his stare. I could feel his presence move closer. Closer. Closer.

I looked through the cracks of the open doors... I could see no one to help me.

In the distance, a patient cleared their throat.

While I continued to retreat and hold onto the trolley, my skin broke out in goosebumps. My feet went cold.

He continued to stare at me.

Why?

I held my breath.

Very quickly, I looked behind and pushed my hand out.

The door did not open. I remembered that Deb had not ordered the hospital key for me.

I looked ahead – he continued to stare at me.

Without looking behind me, I tapped the door.

I had my back on the door. I leaned into it.

It did not budge.

While the trolley blocked us, I could feel his presence on me. I could almost smell him: rotten cabbage, the kind that lay on the top of a batch and spoiled the rest.

Did he need help?

Why did he stare at me?

What happened to all the hospital attendants and nurses?

What about the doctor?

I could feel a panic attack setting in… and, then I heard a *click*.

Minh opened the door.

'You are not supposed to enter this section alone,' she said in surprise. 'Are you okay?'

She looked at a male nurse behind her, and pulled me and the trolley out.

When I dialled again, Emma picked up.

'Hello Emma. How are you today?' I attempted, my voice calm and controlled. 'You told me to check the app five days ago. I usually get regular shifts and suddenly I have no shifts. What is happening? Have I been fired?'

'I told you already. Check the app.' She sighed. 'Bye!'

When the rain started, it pitted and patted consistently but never forcefully; a lull rather than an explosion.

I looked up because several drops tapped my nose. I set buckets and blankets around the house. With no plans for the night, I spent the night on Netflix. I lay vertically on my bed, my hair sliding out of the bed and stared at the screen – it burned my eyes. I absorbed several episodes. I did not think or feel much.

Every hour or so, I emptied the bucket and let it fill up. A cacophony of drops disturbed me through the night – *drip, drop, clip, clap.*

An ochre-coloured stain formed on my ceiling.

I crossed out all the self-care tips: art, journaling, exercise, and meditation. I changed tactics and opened Tinder again.

Everyone looked so happy, so purposeful – their very 'best selves'. Why did people find confidence so attractive? Why did people continue to perpetuate these ploys – it felt so visibly manufactured? What did they hope to achieve?

It had rained earlier in the day. Then the sun came out. The air sparkled, full of illuminated raindrops. We moved to Carlton Gardens. I rolled my scarf around my face and neck. A strand of hair slipped out. He lovingly tucked it back in. We continued to talk and move around, leisurely....

The rain continued to spill onto my nose, I closed my phone and ran for a fresh cloth.

When I returned, I noticed him on the app. He had listed a series of hobbies – books, poetry, and art – and posted holiday pictures.

We had mocked people like this together. Why had he chosen to become one?

With my cloth, I made a light movement to the left and he disappeared.

This time I did not slip into the fantasy of *us*. I fell asleep.

When I arrived at the hospital the next day, Deb ordered me up to Level 10.

What had happened?

Was I promoted?

Was this because of yesterday's 'incident'?

The hospital stationed food attendants on busy floors like Level 10. They stood outside the rooms; and handed out food and collected rubbish. They had tabs to make extra orders for patients. They never visited the kitchen or other floors. At meal-time, attendants brought up hot food trollies.

This was a position that only older attendants had; even Minh had not been promoted to this level. It took years of service to be stationed on a floor.

Floor 10 smelled clean. On top of the lights in the corridor, lamps had been set around the room to create a homey vibe.

I could also hear the busy movement of bodies: nurses moved in and out in a rush; doctors filed papers; and patients moved around the floor.

When Peter met me, he nodded and continued past me.

Most of the time, I did not have much to do.

I stood. Smiled. Stared at the clock.

Then I moved around the floor. I checked rooms.

'Perhaps another cup of tea? Would you like a snack? Would you like your meal heated up?'

'I'm alright. Thank you, dear,' they chimed.

Then I returned to my spot. Straightened my uniform. Stood up. Stood on my toes – the ache in my feet had not subsided.

I robotically smiled at any nurses or doctors. Looked at the clock. Checked my phone. Fifteen minutes had passed.

Then I repeated the cycle.

My shift ended at 8:30 p.m.

When I returned to the kitchen, I looked for Deb. I needed her name on the payment form.

When I found her, she needed a pen so she led me to her office.

'Did you see her lipstick today?' the kitchen attendant from the elevator said. 'She leaned in extra close today.'

'Yes, that shade of pink. Repulsive,' his friend responded. 'She's old enough to be my mum.'

'She's old enough to be your nan, mate... ' the first one responded and chuckled.

Deb heard this and stopped suddenly. They looked astounded at the sight of her. They both smiled at her. She cleared her throat. While humiliation flickered on her face at first, she recovered in seconds; she straightened her posture and made eye contact.

'The freezer needs to be restocked. Get to that as soon as possible,' she said. 'Make sure it's done before the kitchen closes.'

We moved on. When she found her pen, she mumbled:

'I started around your age.'

'Why did you stay?' I asked. We had never had a normal conversation before. She had simply issued orders. I don't think she even remembered my name. She usually just called me 'you'.

'Well, I finished uni, temporarily started here, and then married. Very quickly, I had kids and older parents to take care of. The pay here is good. There's also flexibility. So I stayed. I don't really have a career. There's no point trying anymore.'

She sighed deeply and handed the form to me.

'It's easy to settle here. But there's not much to do.'

I called Emma a couple more times. When she heard my voice, she just cut the line.

Eventually, they suspended my app and I realised I had lost my job.

Devana Senanayake writes short fiction which explores the psyche of her characters and touches on the intersections of race, class, and disability. She is inspired by the rich cultures of the three countries she has lived in thus far: Sri Lanka, Australia, and the UK. Devana remembers the Literary Salon from her days as an exchange student in Scotland. She enjoys her various jobs, mostly as a journalist, some times as a researcher, and occasionally as a radio producer.

Auvers-sur-Oise

Philip Caveney

He had been working on the painting for most of the afternoon, but it wasn't really going to plan. It was a blustery sort of day and the wind was persistently kicking the wheatfield into violent motion, threatening to knock over his rickety easel. He had always been happier in his studio and, if he really had to work outdoors, he preferred the gentler climes of Provence. What's more, there was an unusual number of crows that day, flapping low over the swaying heads of wheat, presumably looking for something to eat.

He tried to manipulate the thick oil paints into the kind of visual agitation he usually excelled at, but this time it simply wasn't working and his gaze kept being drawn to the narrow path that led into the middle of the field. He couldn't stop thinking that perhaps he should abandon the painting and do the thing that he had been considering for so long; he was increasingly convinced that, if he just went ahead with it, he would finally have rest and would no longer have to worry about coaxing out demons and setting them down on unrelenting canvas. He thought about the stacks of unsold paintings back in his workshop and his spirit quailed. His planned renaissance of exploding colours and violent, writhing paint strokes wasn't working out the way he'd hoped. Oh, yes, a few critics had said good things about his work, but nobody seemed to want to own one of his paintings....

And then, quite suddenly, the woman was there, walking out from the middle of the wheatfield. He wondered where she might have come from. She wasn't somebody that he recognised – indeed, she didn't look like anybody from these parts. She was dressed in a strange metallic suit, immodestly close-fitting and adorned with what looked like flexible metallic tubes along the arms and legs. Her black hair was cut unusually short and slicked close around her head.

As she moved closer, the artist noticed that her gaze was fixed on him, a look of recognition in her pale blue eyes. But still he was certain he didn't know her. The woman came around and stood behind him, looking over his shoulder at the painting. She gave off an odd, metallic smell that caught in his throat. He tried to ignore her, thinking that she would soon get bored and walk away. She didn't.

'I've been looking for you,' she said at last. She spoke the local dialect well, he thought, but not perfectly. The voice was too considered, too careful. English? American, perhaps? She was certainly making a decent fist of the language.

'Have you?' he asked, though truth be told, he wasn't really all that interested. 'You're not from round here,' he added, just to make conversation.

'I've come here to meet you,' said the woman. 'I've come a very long way. Further than you'd ever think.'

'Really?' He slashed another black line into the turbulent grey sky on the canvas. The sound of the crows was like a knife stabbing repeatedly into his head.

'Yes. If you want to know the truth, I've come from the future. Many years into the future.'

He resisted rolling his eyes. There were too many people suffering this kind of delusion. He'd met several like her when he was at the hospital in the South, people who, he'd eventually decided, were a lot worse off than him. He'd come North to escape them, but somehow he never could quite shake them off.

She pointed to the canvas. 'I know what's on your mind,' she said. 'I came here to tell you not to lose heart. I know how hard it is for you. I understand your pain.'

Now he turned to look at her. 'Do you really?' he muttered.

'Oh yes. I know all about your life. I have studied it, you see. I have read everything I could find about you. And I came here because I needed to tell you not to give up. Years from now – many years, you understand – your work will be famous. It will be reproduced in posters, books... on fridge magnets.... '

'What's a fridge magnet?' he asked.

'It's hard to explain,' she said. 'But never mind that. I want you to know that your work will be celebrated. The original paintings – pictures like this one – will exchange hands for millions of euros – sorry, francs. *Millions*. Your name will be famous around the world.'

'So... I will be rich?' he asked, feeling something he rarely experienced – a powerful surge of hope.

'Sadly, no. You will not sell another painting in your lifetime. I appreciate that's hard for you to hear, but it doesn't really matter, because long after your death, everyone will know your name. I just wanted to tell you that.' She glanced at the back of her wrist. 'I only have a few moments. There are other people waiting for me, people I need to see. We could only get a window of a few minutes.' She seemed to be thinking hard now. 'It's been a privilege to meet you,' she told him. 'Don't give up,' she added. 'Please. Don't let this be the last painting.'

'Why should it be?' he asked her.

She smiled sadly. And with that she turned and walked briskly back towards the wheatfield. She was half way down the central path when there was a bright flash of light and, as abruptly as she had appeared, she was gone.

So she wasn't real, he thought. Another damned figment. He was beginning to get used to them, but still dreaded them. They scared him, these visions.

He studied the field for a moment. The crows were still flapping low over the waving heads of wheat, their shrieks a shrill cacophony. He considered what the woman had told him. Nonsense, of course. Another product of his overworked imagination. He would be famous. His work would live forever... but he would not sell another painting in his lifetime. Not much of a prospect, any of it.

He sighed and reached under the oil-smeared rags beneath the easel, and found the hard handle of the pistol, just where he had left it. He pulled the gun out and studied it for a moment. With his right hand, he sketched one more dark, ragged shape in the grey sky.

Then he set down the brush and started walking, following the same path that the woman had taken.

He hadn't been sure before, but the woman's words, though undoubtedly gibberish, had somehow helped him make up his mind. He was tired of trying. It was time to be decisive.

For a moment he hesitated. He thought about turning back, adding a few more touches to the painting, but he decided against it. His mind was made up. The picture was finished. It was all finished.

He kept walking, eyes fixed on the path, the cold handle of the gun gripped tightly in his paint-splashed fist.

Philip Caveney knew he wanted to be a writer after reading *Something Wicked This Way Comes* at the age of thirteen. It took him ten years to publish his first novel but, after that, it got a little easier. Writing under his own name, and sometimes as Danny Weston, he now has more than fifty books to his credit. He's won the Scottish Children's Book Award and been nominated for the Carnegie Medal. When he moved to Edinburgh in 2010, he was delighted to discover the Literary Salon. The monthly meetings offer friendship, community, and a sense of belonging.

Looking

JAMES FLOWERDEW

MeetCute®

Julie Galante

because you know what you like

'Welcome to your onboarding session for MeetCute®: the dating service for people who know what they like. I'm Chris, and I'll be introducing you to this exciting new experience! What sets us apart from other virtual reality dating services is simple: rather than choosing your own avatar, you choose one for your date. That way, you get to see exactly who you want to see.'

Greta thought Chris was the most enthusiastic product rep she'd ever seen. The large, curved glass monitor in front of them glowed with images of smiling, impossibly attractive couples. Chris touched a menu icon in the corner of the screen and began swiping through options.

'Let's get you started, shall we? First, you'll read through profiles of the many active users who are waiting to meet someone just like you. You'll find the same type of information you would expect on any other dating site: personality type, career, religion, and so on. You'll note that we here at MeetCute® do not create matches for you. It is our belief that the one who best knows what you want is you! Our technology exists to help you get that.'

Greta's eyes darted around the screen, trying to

keep up with Chris's fingers, which were now scrolling through images of partial human beings.

'Next, you'll browse our head and body library. These are all actual heads and bodies of people in our dating pool, just not necessarily the ones belonging to the people you've selected. Again, you'll be able to filter by several qualifiers: muscular, lanky, or curvy body types, for example. Feel free to bookmark any that you find attractive.

'Once you've matched with a profile, you'll have the opportunity to assign a head and body to that profile, and you'll be able to start exchanging messages. Chat as long or as little as you like – it's all included in the service!'

Greta observed as Chris tapped away at the controls. In the centre of the screen, a parade of heads paired up with a line of bodies in perpetually-changing combinations. It made her dizzy to watch.

'Does anyone ever choose the same person's profile, head, and body, just by chance?' Greta thought that sounded romantic.

'Not yet! We had a couple of two-out-of-three matches happen back in beta when the database was smaller, but never a full set. Once you and a profile match have decided you'd like to meet, you'll pick a time and choose a date experience from our location library. It's as simple as that! Ten hours of date time are included in your current package, and you can always purchase more.'

'Oh, I don't know about that. This whole thing was a gift from some friends – I'm not really sure it's right for me.' Greta let out a small laugh.

'Of course. Many people are unsure when they start using our service, but we have a very high repeat customer

'Right. Wait, does that mean that my face could be matched up to someone else?'

'It could indeed. Your face on someone else's body, inhabited by a completely different person altogether – might be some lucky guy's dream woman.'

Greta wasn't sure she liked the sound of that. 'And these virtual dates – how do they work, exactly? I mean, like eating at a restaurant – is the food virtual, too?'

'Excellent question. You will indeed be presented with real food and drink. Due to the immersive nature of the virtual experience, your brain will think you're eating whatever you see in front of you, even though you're actually consuming a flavourless jelly consisting mainly of potato starch. It's quite impressive, really. You'll swear you're having lobster or steak tartare or whatever it is you ordered. The taste is incredibly real.'

Greta was sceptical but intrigued.

A week later, Greta returned to the MeetCute® facility. After chatting with Sam online for several days, they had agreed on a date.

Once the technician had finished attaching motion sensors to her body, he placed the VR mask over Greta's head. Suddenly, she found herself in a small, nicely-appointed dressing room. She walked over to the full-length mirror and took in the woman she saw: long black hair, dark eyes, a long, sloped nose which came to a cute, upturned point. A slender figure, save for large breasts – much larger than her own – encased in a turquoise dress much tighter than any she owned. It wasn't her, yet somehow she understood it was her, reborn as Sam's dream date.

Looking down, she saw shiny black combat boots – not unlike a pair she frequently wore. At least he'd got one detail right.

She exited the room and found herself at an outdoor cafe in a place that looked a lot like Rome. She saw Sam sitting at one of the little round tables, framed in the rounded archway of a portico. He stood up to greet her as she walked over.

'Nice to meet you.' Greta giggled.

'Pleasure.' Sam extended his virtual hand to shake hers. Greta noticed a shiny red manicure on her own hand as she went through the motions of the greeting.

They sat down and Greta took in their surroundings. Across from them in the square, families were chatting and eating gelato. Water from a tall stone fountain glistened in the sunlight. A couple on a powder-blue vespa whizzed by on the cobbled street.

A waiter came to take their order, after which Greta turned her attention to Sam.

'Have you done this before?' she asked.

'A few times, yes. This your first?'

'It is. So – how different do you look from what I chose for you?' Greta admired her handiwork. She'd never been on a date with anyone quite so muscly before. And that cleft chin! Perfect.

'I don't really bother to look at the avatars dates choose for me. It seems rather irrelevant, doesn't it?'

'I – I don't know. I was quite interested to see what you had chosen. Maybe it tells me something about you? I notice we both selected dark hair for each other.'

Sam shrugged. 'I wouldn't read too much into it. Just enjoy the opportunity to date someone you find physically attractive.'

'Right.' Greta looked down and tried to twirl some of her sleek, long hair around a finger. She found she could not.

The waiter reappeared with their drinks – a Peroni for Sam, a prosecco for Greta. They raised their glasses in a toast but had to forgo the satisfying clink.

The rest of the two hours (MeetCute® recommended an initial date of no more than two hours) flew by, Sam and Greta chatting about bands, jobs, pets, and mothers. They agreed that music sounded more authentic on vinyl, and people who owned ferrets were not to be trusted.

'I'd like to see you again,' said Sam, leaning in to kiss Greta. She was surprised not to be able to feel his lips against hers and then felt silly for having forgotten.

'That would be nice.' She blushed, wondering if her avatar had as well.

'Those other MeetCute dates you went on before me – did they have the same head and body that I do?' They were strolling in a grove of redwoods on a very sunny day. Dappled light illuminated the dirt path through the giant trees. The MeetCute® facilitator had warned her to stick to the path.

'No, not exactly. At first, I tried out a variety of looks. In fact, I gave the first woman I went out with a totally different head each time I saw her. MeetCute doesn't recommend that, but it was an efficient way for me to figure out what I really wanted. Since then, I've only ever made minor adjustments.'

Glancing upwards into the branches of one of the trees, Greta wondered if she had been minorly adjusted. She made a mental note to check next time she encountered a mirror. 'So, what are you really wearing?' she asked.

'What?'

'In real life – what do you have on right now?' For their date, Greta had dressed him in a dark blue polo shirt and chinos. The shirt's colour brought out his eyes.

'Oh, that. Um, Atari t-shirt and cargo shorts?'

Greta found this answer vaguely disappointing. 'Doesn't sound like you made much of an effort.'

'But you can't see me.'

'Does that matter?'

'Isn't it the whole point? What I look like is irrelevant.'

Greta didn't know what to say to that.

'Do people ever meet in real life?' Greta asked the MeetCute® technician who was removing her VR gear after the date.

'Oh, we don't recommend that. I'm sure some have, but I've never heard of any success stories coming from it.'

'What success stories do you hear in general?' Greta was trying to imagine what would make a VR relationship successful. Virtual wedding? Virtual kids?

'What? Oh, you know. People are just happy to continue to use our service. We've been recording testimonials for the website – give those a watch. MeetCute® has some very enthusiastic fans! That's you all sorted for now. See you at your next session.'

'But wouldn't you like to meet in real life someday?' Greta asked over dinner at a swish NYC sushi bar.

'We'd only end up disappointed. Why mess up a good thing?'

'But couldn't it possibly make things even better – our connection more intense, more real?'

The chef placed a long, narrow dish of sashimi in front of them.

'MeetCute Version 2.0 is supposed to have new features that will make everything seem more real. Touch, for example. That will definitely deepen our connection. Plus, that way you don't have to see how disappointing I look in real life.'

'How do you know I'd be disappointed?'

'What are the chances you wouldn't be? I mean, the me you see now, you picked out for yourself.'

Greta admired the phoenix tattoo on Sam's left forearm, which she had added earlier that day. 'Yes. But – I don't need you to be perfect.'

'Let's think about it.' Sam picked up a pink slice of sashimi and popped it into his mouth.

'At the very least it will save money, not having to pay MeetCute for all our dates!' Greta said, picking up the bottle of chianti and refilling both their glasses.

They had returned to Italy for their fifth date – a cozy restaurant somewhere vaguely southern. Checked tablecloths, a mural of an olive grove, bowls of citrus fruits – bright green leaves still attached.

She'd need to buy more MeetCute® time if she wanted to see him again.

'It's cheaper than flying to another country every time we meet.' Sam grinned and took a sip of wine.

'I don't have to see you in other countries. We could just, you know, go to the pub or something.'

'We can do that via MeetCute, too. There are pages of pubs to choose from in the location catalogue.'

Greta was determined to get Sam to see things her way. 'But aren't you… curious? Don't you want to see the real me?'

Sam put down his fork and gazed at her.

'You look very real to me.'

'You look very real to me, too. But we know this isn't real.' Greta reached out and put her hand through his chest to illustrate her point.

'Why does that matter so much to you?'

'Why does it matter so little to you?'

'It would just complicate things. The real world is a messy place.'

'Sometimes messy can be fun.'

'Maybe. Let's enjoy our pasta.' Sam made a flourish of twirling his *spaghetti alle vongole* onto his fork.

Greta: Wait, how will we recognise each other? Should we exchange photos? Describe ourselves?

Sam: I'll wear a green hat.

Greta was nervous but excited that she had finally talked Sam into it. She knew they would have a connection. They already did.

What should she wear? Given what Sam had been dressing her in, he'd prefer her in something tight, with cleavage, but that wasn't really her. She leafed through her closet once more, wondering if she should have dyed her hair darker.

Greta's heart sank. Sam looked nothing like the tall, muscular, tattooed avatar she had chosen for him. Maybe this had been a terrible mistake. She was having a hard time making eye contact. He kept looking down, causing his hat to obscure most of his acne-riddled face. It came as a relief to her when he suggested some tequila shots. After two, or maybe three, conversation started to flow. If she closed her eyes, it almost felt the same as their previous dates. Yes, this was the same man, the one whose company she had enjoyed in Italy, and New York, and all those other places. And the place didn't matter, not really. She wanted to know him here, now, in the present. In real life. People around them were probably saying they were mismatched, with her looking so done-up and him in a t-shirt and jeans, but who cared what people thought?

Sam was gone when Greta woke up the next morning. Her memory of the end of the evening was a bit fuzzy, but the scenes that did show up – awkward fumbling, kisses involving too many teeth – caused a cringe to creep up her shoulders. With a groan she rolled over and reached for her phone on the bedside table. There was a message from Sam.

Sam: I was going to suggest we go back to MeetCute dates, but tbh I'm not sure it would work for me – the integrity of that world has been compromised. It was an interesting experiment you talked me into, tho. Thx for that.

Greta: Wait, you don't want to see me anymore at all? I'm sorry I was so taken aback at the beginning of the evening. I can learn to live with the real you, I think. Couldn't we just try it again?

Greta wasn't that shallow, was she? No. She would prove as much to herself and to Sam. She would see this through. She felt sweat prickling at her armpits as she awaited his reply.

Sam: I don't think that's a good idea.

Greta: Why???

Sam: You're a great girl. It's just not going to work.

Greta: Seriously? What changed? I'm the same person you've been dating all this time.

She stared at the screen. Several minutes passed with no reply. She messaged again.

Greta: You could at least tell me why.

She stared some more. Finally, the little dots popped up to indicate Sam was typing. They appeared and disappeared several times before his response came.

Sam: Your tits are just way too small. Sry.

Julie Galante explores relationships, the uncanny, identity, and grief in her fiction and creative non-fiction. For her, writing is a way to make sense of the world and to forge connections with others – she enjoys being able to make people laugh or see something in a different way through her work. She loves living in a city with such a thriving and welcoming literary community, including the Literary Salon. Julie is also a visual artist – her paintings and mixed media pieces often inspire her writing (and vice versa).

My Antony

Susan Nickalls

You appeared as if by magic one day towards the end of summer. Standing ankle deep in the Water of Leith, buck naked with smooth pennies for nipples and not a wisp of hair; you resembled a great bronze river god. You gazed towards Powderhall Bridge, arms slightly tensed, hands poised in perpetual anticipation, your head cocked to one side. Were you listening out for a stray billy goat trip-trap-trip-trapping over the nearby wooden bridge, or angling to catch a slippery trout?

These questions intrigued me as I passed you on my daily lunchtime strolls that liberated my brain from the computer and my body from the house. Although common sense told me otherwise, I often experienced a nanosecond flutter of doubt when I approached, the way the stomach lurches on catching sight of a lover. Placed quite low down in the river, you remained hidden by clumps of weeds until I was within reach of the bridge. Only then did I start to breathe again when I glimpsed your bronze head. For despite your inertia, you are transformed every day by the infinite combinations of weather and light.

I wonder what you made of your first snow at the end

of November, falling before the colour had faded from the frozen autumn leaves. Twinkling like diamonds in the sun, the icy crystals reminded me of the toothpaste-white dazzle from the snowy photographs in a childhood book, *Teddy Edward's Winter Holiday*. But while the snowflakes had smothered most of the landscape, they provided you with scant clothing. At most a jumper slung casually over your shoulders or an ermine collar topped by a matching zucchetto. On one occasion you even sported a Gorbachev-like sickle on your brow. Sometimes these luminous splatterings were the only way of distinguishing you from winter's ubiquitous greyness.

As the temperatures plummeted below zero you acquired a sleek, transparent surfboard of ice, so that when the snow thawed and the water levels rose I thought you might have surfed down the Water of Leith or gone swimming. But no, you were still there; your head and shoulders just visible above the waterline, protected by a shawl of twigs and other debris. By the next day this had shrunk to a small island at your feet, the water only just licking your shins.

With constant activity to distract you, I had to admire your unwavering focus, although I secretly suspected you noticed more than you let on. The brazen fox stalking a duck in broad daylight right behind your back, the turquoise flash of a kingfisher zipping upriver. What did you make of the wagging school boys furtively having a toke under the bridge? They thought they were invisible, completely unaware that the sickly-sweet aroma and coils of smoke were a dead give-away. As for the two girls on a sledge careering downhill to splosh at your feet after a mischievous boy gave them a good shove; I'm sure I caught the outline of a smirk on your lips as one of the bedraggled girls stomped up the hill, castigating her friends with, 'I cannae believe none of youse videoed it.'

Certainly, since your arrival, traffic on the path has increased as people stop to look, point, and take photos of you. My protectiveness towards you surprised me, as did my strong sense of ownership. It was about this time that you went, at least in my mind, from being Gormley IV to My Antony. Visitors to the house would be asked, 'Have you seen My Antony?' If weather and shoes permitted they were then given a private view. Then there are the dog walkers, including a blind man from the nearby flats who walks to the end of the bridge mirroring your stance, his head tilted and arms at his sides, as his ears monitor the progress of his self-exercising Alsatian.

Very quickly you became a familiar landmark on my route, like the heron at the weir and the parallel lines of cherry trees holding hands across the brae near St Mark's Park. So it was a shock one day to find you had vanished. It was the talk of the dog walkers and even speculated upon in the Broughton Spurtle. I dismissed the possibility of theft given that it would take a serious amount of heavy lifting to uproot goodness knows how many tonnes of you. By now I had discovered your other doppelgangers in the 6 TIMES series along the river. Had you all been collectively summoned to worry Manhattanites from the edge of rooftops or paddle in Norwegian fjords? Had you fallen over? Peering into the river's murky depths revealed only myself in fragments. But I was on the right track.

After three Antony-absent days, I contacted the National Galleries of Scotland and spoke rather uncannily to Michael Gormley – no relation – who reassured me you had just taken a lengthy dive. Apparently you have a hinge at your base which topples you over when the currents run too fast. I sighed with relief and waited. And waited.

It was nearly a month before you appeared again. By chance the time of my walk happened to coincide with your resurrection. What a palaver that was. There were four divers in the murky water attaching wires and chains to you as a generator loudly hummed encouragement. After forty minutes or so, the gigantic crane squeezed into a small grassy space between the riverbank and the flats, raised its long arm. And very slowly, up you came; reborn with a rusty marble patina, courtesy of the riverbed. A sculpture for all seasons rightfully restored to nature's expansive and ever-changing public gallery, you are, once again, My Antony.

Susan Nickalls started her love affair with words and ideas at a young age, around the same time she started piano lessons. Since then, writing and music have combined to form the heart of her creative work. Buoyed by the encouragement from writers at the Literary Salon, Susan recently started her first novel while completing an MA in Creative Writing. She admires Katherine Mansfield and Nora Ephron, and reveres T.S. Eliot. In her dreaming reality, she is an astronaut who writes, sings, and tap dances in space.

Art of Ariadne

Lyndsey Croal

Inspired by Titian's 'Bacchus and Ariadne', 1522-3

Peace was often brought by retribution, but the payment demanded by my father, after the murder of my brother, was particularly cruel. Every seasonal cycle by Minos's decree, fourteen Athenian men and women – the strongest and fairest of their land – would arrive at the harbour of Knossos. Presented like lambs to slaughter, they would face Asterion, my ungodly half-brother, who resided in the labyrinthine prison beneath our palace.

After the first two cycles, I longed for the day when one of the sacrifices would conquer the labyrinth and end Asterion's tragic existence. But no one that stepped foot in the maze ever returned. Soon the twisting halls were littered with bones, and the echoes of screams. The minotaur was not so easily defeated.

I often dreamt of the sacrifices, their lost souls visiting me on their journey to the underworld. Some told me of the pain they'd endured. Others of the family, loves, or hopes they left behind at home. Each year, I pleaded with my father to end the needless bloodshed, Asterion's suffering, and to spare the Athenians. But he would not be persuaded. Once terms of surrender had been agreed, they could not be broken. To do so would be a sign of weakness, and if there was anything my father hated, it was looking weak. That, and my mother.

*

The third cycle came around as the spring weather stilled the crystal blue sea and seabirds returned from their migration south. The clanging of ships could be heard from the harbour, alongside the screeches of gulls and the squawking of merchants. In the midst was the familiar three-tone bell that signalled the Athenians had arrived.

I headed to the main hall, where I took my seat dutifully by my mother's side. She was regal, as always, long auburn hair falling in loose curls down her back so that she almost glowed in the afternoon light. Her face was carved into a scowl, as it had been since Asterion had been torn from her, but her green eyes were alert and sharp, readied for the difficult day ahead. I was starting to look more like her as palace life wore me down and the same sharpness showed on my face. I wondered if the palace servants saw us as the same; tight-lipped women under Minos's control, blessed with the beauty of the Gods. At least I didn't look like my father who joined us shortly after. Half-drunk, half-naked, with one of his mistresses hanging off his arm. My mother didn't flinch, sitting there poised and silent as stone. Not even when the girl let out a squeal of delight as my father called for more wine.

Gods, I hated him. Sprawled out on his throne, greasy hair gleaming in the morning light, and wine running down his throat; he had the grace and manners of a mule. He was greying too, the wrinkles beneath his eyes growing more and more twisted as the months passed. He told anyone who would listen that he got his orders directly from Zeus himself, but I knew no deity spoke in his favour anymore. Betraying Poseidon had its consequences, and ours lived beneath our feet. Now our home and everyone within spitting distance was suffering.

My parents wouldn't let me leave this place. I was the only one that could tame my half-brother after all. The only one he would allow close without descending into a violent rage. Every week I'd speak to him behind safe walls or sing to him through iron bars, as he sat cross-legged, huffing out breath slowly. I'd tell him about my week, the same monotonous routines, confined as I was by my parents' overprotectiveness – Gods forbid they lose another child. When I mentioned my occasional visits to see Daedalus, Asterion's breathing would still as if he knew I spoke of the man who'd built his prison. I wondered what he spent his time thinking of. Freedom, flesh, blood? It was an awful fate to spend life in such darkness with a deep hunger that could never be sated.

While Asterion lived, I had no hope of true freedom. Neither of us did. So, I devised a plan. First, I had returned to the lessons my aunt had given me when she had come to help my mother birth my half-brother – at the time I'd been too naïve to really understand her power, but now I had begun to. I spent many a night weaving threads of gold and experimenting with tonics and enchantments. It had taken a long time to feel confident enough in my abilities, but for this cycle, I was ready.

The footsteps echoed across the stillness of the throne room as the fourteen tributes came to stand before us. Most were hunched over, no longer the strongest and fairest of any land. Their eyes were fixed on the floor, or on the shackles around their wrists, accepting the will of the Fates. Pity and shame tugged at my stomach, but I was used to swallowing my feelings. I eyed the group carefully, measuring their statures, calculating their potential, and caught the eye of one. He stood taller than the rest, staring at me with piercing blue eyes, his posture defiant. Though he was slim, I could see the strength in his arms and the intelligence in his stare. His was the soul of a hero, one who would not give in to his fate easily. I felt my mouth curve into a half-smile.

My father began the ritual, padding up and down the row. Eventually, he descended into his usual speech, though his words were slurred and muddled.

'Here y'are, fair Athenians, to pay retribution, for' – he shook his fist in the air – 'for taking m'son, Androgeos, dearest, noble, strongest of m'blood, taken t'soon, from... you will meet monster beneath, t'answer for crimes, such crimes, I.... ' His hand lurched to the mistress at his side, and she steadied him with an insolent giggle. I rolled my eyes. He didn't even have the decency to show an ounce of respect. Or regret.

I stood and walked over to the company. 'Father, why not let me finish the ritual? Let your handmaiden take you to clean up.'

His mistress flinched at the title, eyes flickering with hate, but she wouldn't dare speak back to me. If I wanted, I could have her removed from the palace.

My father looked at me with one eye shut then let out a short laugh. 'Come, come, not needed. Let the... what is it... begin.'

He grabbed the bottle of wine with one hand, and his mistress with another, and they stumbled out of the room together. The tributes quivered before me, almost looking as though they had half a foot in the underworld already. All except for the blue-eyed one who wore a fixed smile.

'Walk,' I ordered, then gestured to the guards to lead the group in a line, with me at the back, just behind Blue-eyes.

When enough distance was between us and the guards, I walked by his side. 'Your name?'

He looked at me, a glimmer in his eyes. 'Theseus.'

'Theseus,' I repeated. 'You will be the first to enter the labyrinth.'

'I would have it no other way,' he agreed, holding up his hands, chains clinking. 'Princess Ariadne.'

'You are here to kill my half-brother?'

If he was surprised at my directness it didn't show. 'Yes.'

'And how do you plan to do that?'

'I am the greatest soldier in Athens.'

Arrogant. Good. 'It won't be enough.'

'We'll see.'

I walked a few more paces. 'I could help you.'

He arched an eyebrow. 'Why would you help me? This is a trick.'

I pulled out the box I'd hidden in my pouch and opened it so he could peer in at the glittering gold contents. 'This thread is seeded with magic,' I explained. 'Cast it at Asterion, and he will fall into a deep sleep. Then you may take care of him. It will be painless and peaceful, for everyone involved.'

He let out a short laugh. 'I need no tricks. I'll kill him how I plan to.'

'No, you won't. For if you do it any other way then you

will die. And if you refuse my gift, I will kill you for your disrespect, while you are bound and at my mercy.'

His shoulders tensed, as if unaccustomed to being threatened. 'I suppose I have no choice but to do as you ask then,' he answered through gritted teeth.

'As you journey into the labyrinth, lay the thread behind you, then you may use it to lead you back to the palace after the deed is done.'

That sparked his interest. 'What's in this for you?'

I smiled. 'After, we will take a ship with your crew and escape this cursed place.'

His lip curled as he weighed up his options. 'A trapped princess that wants an adventure. How novel.'

I resisted the urge to slap him in his smug jaw. Instead, I took the delicate thread out of the box and tucked it into his tunic. As I did, I saw a glint of a dagger. I'd made the right choice.

*

The docks were busy with the bustle of people. Hooded and cloaked as I was, none would know that a princess was in their midst. I stood on the pier with the ship I'd arranged behind me, half a crew on board. My friend, Daedalus, was shouting orders to them, readying them for a voyage. After, he joined me on the pier.

'You are sure about this, Ariadne?' He said my name in a whisper.

'I cannot stay here any longer. This place is poison.'

He nodded in agreement. 'The crew is ready to sail at first order if Theseus comes.'

'When he comes.'

He nodded again, though I could feel his uncertainty. Why was I putting so much faith in a mortal man?

Maybe I should have done the deed myself. Although if it had come to it, I'm not sure I'd have been able to. Monster though he was, Asterion was still of my blood.

A crowd was moving towards us, laughter and jubilation piercing the air. One voice cried, 'the beast is dead!'

My breath caught. Theseus was striding towards me with the rest of the Athenians at his side. He caught my eye and smiled.

'Princess Ariadne!' He exclaimed, and before I could stop him, he had run across the pier and lifted me in the air. 'My dearest love, I have rescued you from the monster.'

Perplexed, I gripped his arms for balance. He spun me around, and I caught sight of the golden thread around his neck, twisted into a sparkling pendant. His tunic was spattered with blood, but I pushed the image of Asterion away. If Theseus had done what I'd said, he wouldn't have suffered.

'Is this our ship? It is beautiful, my love. Come, let us sail the seas together and celebrate our victory. May Poseidon bless our voyage.' He took my hand and led me to the deck, where he took a deep breath, as if trying to taste the sea air. Daedalus followed next to me, looking as confused as I felt.

'Was it you that helped my dearest Ariadne?' Theseus asked him.

'It was. And I hope this ship serves you well.' Daedalus gave me a look.

'Thank you. You've been a great friend. I'll miss you,' I whispered to him.

He squeezed my arm. 'Be careful. It seems Theseus

has developed an unusual attachment to you.' He lowered his voice, and added, 'Go along with it at least until you're safe? Promise me that?'

I smiled despite myself. 'Yes, you have always been wise.' I hugged him, then took one last look at the city behind me. The palace loomed like a shadow. I whispered goodbye to Asterion and stepped aboard the vessel. I signalled for Theseus and the freed crew to set sail and stood at the deck watching until my friend was just a dot on the horizon.

*

We sailed for weeks, the seas kind and welcoming. Theseus set a course for Athens, but he left the navigation to his crew. Most of his time was spent with me, sitting as close as possible, playing with my hair, promising me gifts, and showering me with compliments. Never had I been shown such attention in my sheltered life, and I won't lie and say part of me didn't like it. But I knew it was ill-gained, so I couldn't find it within myself to return his affections. Nor did I want to live my life tied to a man because I'd made a mistake with a spell. It would be like going from one prison to another.

One afternoon I asked if I could see the golden thread, as I assumed it was to blame for his sudden affection – the enchantment I'd laid upon it was only supposed to affect Asterion, but I wasn't as practiced in magic as my aunt and mother. Maybe I'd created an accidental binding to Theseus after he'd carried out my request. As I suspected, as I leant for it his eyes flashed and he lurched away, hands clutching it to his chest.

We soon stopped at the isle of Naxos for respite. Sandy beaches and yellow cliffs greeted us, and we disembarked to set up camp. Theseus sent out hunters and gatherers to restock, and others to collect wood to repair parts of the weatherworn ship.

We were to stay for three days, then we'd be on our way to Athens, our final destination. I knew I didn't belong with the people there. Even if I had helped their hero, I was the daughter of their enemy. Theseus could only do so much to protect me, and though he'd been kind to me, it wasn't of his own free will. What would happen to me if the spell broke?

As Theseus was overseeing repairs, I set off on my own to hike the island, enjoying the lightness of the air, the warmth, and the freedom. I soon came upon a pool in a valley nestled between a grove of orange trees and grapevines full to bursting. Unable to resist, I slipped my clothes off and jumped in. As I lay floating on the water, gazing up at the sunshine, a voice came from behind me.

'Let me guess, here to seek the will of Dionysus?'

I scrambled out and looked around. Then I saw him, a figure lying on a bench between the vines. I pulled my dress on hastily and ventured over to him. Up close he was beautiful, his skin radiant, and his thick brown curls knotted with red leaves. In his hand was a chalice of wine, and across his body was a lazily draped tunic covering only one shoulder. I had rarely met the Gods in my life, but I knew I was looking at one.

'I'm sorry to disturb you,' I said. 'This spot is beautiful.'

'I could say the same about my new company.' He sat up. 'You truly didn't know I was here?'

I shook my head, then pointed down the cliff to the shore where our ship was anchored. 'We're only stopping off on our way to Athens. Theseus is our captain.'

He tilted his head as if to get a better look at me. 'But it is by your will that you are here, is it not, Princess?'

I smiled softly. 'In a way.'

He stood and approached me languidly. Something bubbled in my stomach, nerves, excitement, yearning. 'You have the blood and power of gods within you. But your family... they took you for granted.'

'I'm not like them.'

'No.' He had a kind smile. 'You are so much more. I must know all of it.' He placed a delicate hand on my cheek and I leant into his touch.

'Theseus would kill you if he saw you touch me,' I said. 'He thinks he owns me.'

'Does he?'

'No.'

'Then I care not.'

I sighed. 'It's not his fault. I cast a spell on him... unintentionally.'

'Then you must cast another to break it.' He led me to sit on the bench next to him and summoned another chalice as if from nowhere.

'How can I make him forget his attachment to me?'

'Maybe that's something I can help with.'

I looked into his eyes. 'What's in it for you?'

He laughed. 'If he forgets you, then maybe you can stay here with me.' He twisted a curl of my hair around his finger, and unlike when Theseus did it, I felt a warmth spread across my body, building like fire. 'If you desire it.'

I took his hand. 'I could be persuaded. What do you have in mind?'

*

That night, I woke Theseus. 'I have something to show you.'

His eyes lit up and of course he followed me.

I led him gently up the hill to the pool, and all the while he asked me eagerly where we were going and told me that I looked even more magnificent at night.

At the pool, I gestured to him to step in, then I ventured to the bench where Dionysus, from his hiding spot, handed me the chalice of wine. I poured the golden tonic I'd created with the grapes from Dionysus's vine inside it and brought it into the pool.

Theseus drank without hesitation, and we sat there together watching the stars dance. With each sip, his words started to slur, and his eyes lost their glow. The compliments stopped coming and he no longer reached for me. When the chalice was drained, it was as if he was looking straight through me, like he had forgotten I existed. I waved a hand in front of his eyes but he didn't react, so I lifted the golden thread from his neck. I dropped it in the pool, and it dissolved into glittering sediment.

As the sun began to rise, he left the pool and wandered back down the path without another word to me.

Together, Dionysus and I climbed to the highest point of Naxos. By the time we reached the top, Theseus and his crew were sailing off towards the dawn.

I pulled Dionysus into an embrace, inhaling his scent. It was as if I'd been wrapped in the finest silk, and for the first time in my life I felt truly free.

'Ariadne,' he said my name softly, savouring every syllable. 'Together we will rule the stars.'

Lyndsey Croal writes speculative or fantastical fiction, set on the edge of the world or in other worlds entirely. Last year, she received a Scottish Book Trust New Writers Award, which she hopes will help towards her dream of one day seeing her books in a bookshop. Since venturing into the Literary Salon a few years ago, she has appreciated the warm welcome given to new and established authors alike. She enjoys reading, gaming, playing music, and tending to her slightly out-of-control plant collection.

The Hopes Which Keep Us Human

Stuart A. Paterson

Snapshots, appetisers, urgent
listings of commonality,
the measured, nervous insanity
beaconing these new beginnings...

I gather them here on a small rock
by the Solway, hour on hour of whispered
trust & talk as night tides into
early day, insistent disbelieving touch
& stroke of necessary solid proof,
the hopes which make us human.

Today you're elsewhere, washed out by another
tide less gentle than the one which
lips my boots, the marker lights so distant
that perhaps they've dipped from sight
beyond the line of our horizon.

This will pass, dark skyline reappear,
the far red lamps of Robin Rigg
wink their promises of soon,
new tide arriving in its half-heard movements
of the hopes which keep us human.

Robin Rigg — wave energy farm between
Galloway & Cumbria in the Solway Firth

Stuart A. Paterson considers Edinburgh his second home, having long-standing connections to the Scottish Poetry Library and Edinburgh's publishing communities. Writing in Scots and English, his poetry explores themes of national and local identities, and sometimes, unashamedly, love. A native of Ayrshire living in remote Galloway, his hobbies and interests include stravaiging those landscapes to which we should all have physical and cultural access.

A WORLD
WORTH
LIVING IN

THE ONE IN CHARGE HAS FALLEN ASLEEP ON THE JOB.
IT'S BEEN TOO PEACEFUL TOO LONG.

HE HAS INDULGED, GROWN COMPLACENT.

THE BOUNTY ACCUMULATES.
TOO MUCH. UNSHARED.
THOSE LEFT UNFETTERED
GORGE THEMSELVES ON WEALTH AND POWER.

THEIR HEADY HIGHS START A FIRE — A BURNING SCOURGE OF INJUSTICE AND PAIN.

THEY ARE DEAF TO THE WORDS OF WARNING. THEY DO NOT CARE TO SEE THE LIGHTS.
WOULD RATHER SEE THEM OBSCURED THAN ADMIT THEY COULD DO WRONG.

THEY DESERVE THIS, THEY SAY.
THEY'VE EARNED IT.
PEOPLE OUGHT TO BE GRATEFUL.

THEY KNOW, DEEP DOWN,
THAT THEY'RE EVADING JUSTICE.
THEY THINK IT'S TOO LATE TO MAKE THINGS RIGHT,
THAT THE WAY OF THINGS IS SET
FOREVER IN THEIR FAVOUR.

THEY ARE WRONG.

THE WORLD'S
REBIRTH AWAITS,
IN EVERY SECOND
OF EVERY DAY.

ALL IT TAKES IS A NUDGE,
A REMINDER.
THE CYCLE ISN'T FUTILE,
IT'S A LESSON,
MEANT TO BE LEARNED
AGAIN AND AGAIN.

THEY BEGIN THE HARDEST TASK: TO IMAGINE A WORLD WORTH LIVING IN.

Natalie Rowland enjoys fantasy and whimsy. When she's not drawing colourful characters, she enjoys going on bike rides and playing games. She'll often discuss the craft of stories with her husband, and when she met a Literary Salon attendee in Leith who told her it was the place to go for inspiring talks, she went!

Walking in Snow

Tracey S. Rosenberg

I am learning how to walk in snow again,
how to find a safe road without cracking
the pale ice puddles. I'm wary
of each frozen foot,
the treachery of whiteness suffocating
every possible fall, this unsalted ground rising
to the soles of my brown boots.
I fear the slip and the sickened
loss of balance before the trip
down, too hard to bear.

I cannot stride. My legs no longer trust.
I hobble and mince. No comforting echo
of *thump, thump*. I chose these boots
the better to keep up with you when we ran
over fields, skimming low together, forcing
   the ice
to lift us into flight.

Now you scatter salt along your path
not to melt snow, but to drive me back.
I wrench an icicle from your corner eaves,
test my weight on this inflexible staff,
beg for its help to keep me whole.

I am walking in snow, slowly.
I have not fallen yet.
I can almost distinguish, under the toes of
    my boots,
the difference between ice and salt.

Tracey S. Rosenberg is the author of a novel and three poetry collections, mostly recently *Secondary* (Red Squirrel Press, 2019), which she completed thanks to a New Writers Award from the Scottish Book Trust. She began attending the Literary Salon way back in the day, and misses the camaraderie and sandwiches. She was a field performer at the closing ceremonies of the 2014 Commonwealth Games. She's currently Writer in Residence at the University of Edinburgh.

Rez (Hugh MacDiarmid)

Ricky Monahan Brown

Maria picked at the shreds of cold, wet fabric and sticky red-brown flesh caked around the leather strap. Then she peeled the strap away from her shoulder and gazed, as if for the first time, at the deep rut it had left in her shoulder. Months had passed since she had first heaved her heavy load, and in all that time, she had never stopped to consider the toll it had taken on her. Now the rut mirrored the trench that the colossal stone foot had ploughed all the way from their point of origin into the long, loping slope falling away before her.

The foot had carved in her a deep echo of her path for hundreds upon hundreds of miles, through sand dunes and soil, valleys and woods. She gingerly examined the wound. Was it because of tiredness that she couldn't feel her shoulder? Was it the cutting-off of her circulation? The vague sensation of discomfort she felt was worse than pain. She knew pain. Uncertainty niggled. Was this muffled feeling the agony of gagged nerves screaming? No matter, it was all fixable. Most things were, in the end.

Sitting heavily on the ground and pressing the tight muscles of her back against the foot, Maria's head came up to the top of its big toe. Above her, the cheekbones of the sky were brushed with a pink blush. Beyond that strip of cloud, a Tyrian purple beautifully bruised the gloaming.

Her father had written to her of the beauty of this scene. He and his brothers and their comrades had drowned at sea returning from the advance voyage. Upon receiving the awful news, the townspeople had erected a monument to the men; demolished now, of course. Yet the remnant of the memorial had gained a power to move as a palimpsest that it could never have had in its original state.

It was, in fact, their father's and their uncles' absence that had sealed Maria and Mo's final decision. With no future for the family left in their old home, they would complete the elders' journey for them. When the time came, Maria had stuffed some essentials in a bag: a length of utility cord, a firelighter, a water bottle and camping cook set, enough dried food to get through the first three days, a single change of clothes, a large, thin piece of fabric that served as a cloth and a towel, and the sturdy, folding utility blade that she had used to cut off handfuls of her hair on the second day.

There was no time or space for anything of sentimental value. In her pocket, she kept her lucky marble, the one she used to roll in her palm when she and her colleagues were running stress tests. They would gather in the control room with only the correct operation of assemblies of control rods standing between them and the awesome, destructive power of a small star, the marble speeding around in her hand to send hard, heavy bad luck to the extremities to be separated out and discarded.

Maria affectionately stroked the foot. 'Thanks,' she said. 'That feels better.' And then, 'We're here now. Here, we build a new life.'

Underneath the pied sky, away down the slope, Maria saw a man approaching. His head was wreathed in the smoke of a cigarette as he traced the path of the old high street that had once carried people and goods from the port, past stores and streets that bore names from all over the world. Now it was pitted and rutted, and vacant lots yawned where the stores used to sit. Maria watched the man carefully and palmed her knife. As he came closer and the smoke cleared in the light breeze, his head resolved into something rugged, monumental, as if his face were hewn from granite. As the last yards between them crumbled, a smile split his face in two.

'Hullo,' he said. 'Would you like a cigarette?'

Maria blanched as he proffered the packet, one stick poking out from the rest. She had seen too many smiling men on her long journey.

'Please. Take one. Do you remember when people used to be able to give and receive cigarettes as little gifts?'

She hesitated; then, remembering those days, took the cigarette with the hand that did not conceal a blade.

'Thank you.'

The man nodded, sparked a heavy brass lighter with a flick of his fingers, and leaned down to light her smoke.

When the pungent taste of lighter fluid had dissipated, the flavour of the tobacco was rich and sweet, like chocolate. A relief after the smokes of her travels: waterlogged and dried out, waterlogged and dried out again. Maria told herself that she wasn't thinking about genes that had already begun to mutate, their critical functions showing the first signs of alteration and malfunction. Instead, she gratefully filled her lungs and remembered her father leaning against a wall, watching her play with her brother. The way he would take a long drag on his cigarette and close his eyes, utterly content. How he would amuse the children, blowing smoke rings, or partially exhaling before pulling the smoke back into his mouth. Doing a ghost, father had called it. Years later, after he had left, Maria and Mo would practice the trick in the cold of the long nights and remember those sunny days.

'What's this?' the man asked, indicating the huge foot.

'It is a little gift. Or a large one.' Maria smiled. 'It is a token from my home town. The man whose foot it was once rescued my town and freed it from the tyrant's yoke. So, I brought it when I joined the exodus, to protect this city.'

Maria had been the one to tell her father of this place first, after she had learned of it from one of her colleagues in the lab. The pictures Eilidh had painted of her home had planted in Maria a desire to journey there and meet its people. She had told Maria of the old city walls that had regulated the town's booming trade and been a deterrent to smugglers but had been no defence against latter-day empire builders.

'But they left us once they had taken everything they wanted,' Eilidh had said. 'And when they left, that was all that we needed.'

Now Maria told the man about her home and about how, when she was a child, its valleys had overflowed with wheat and vegetables and vineyards and olive groves. She told him about the badlands that had once been separate from the places where the people had lived and farmed. But after the terror, the bones of the dead had mixed with clay and chalk and sandstone and pushed barren soil into the towns. The hard rains that came once a year had whipped the towns into canyons and plateaus and isolated hills and dark valleys.

The man told her about how he had read, 200 million years ago, the land where she now sat had been a desert. And as that land had roamed the globe, it had become polar and tropical and temperate. Some of the passengers had been tossed overboard along the way, he explained, deemed to be of less value than the livestock for whom their land had been cleared, of less value than the timber for which the old forests had been levelled.

'Yet along the way, other travellers joined the trek,' he continued. 'You've come a long way. You must be tired. And hungry. Please, will you eat with my partner and I tonight? He can do wonderful things with seafood.'

Despite her gnawing hunger, Maria's instinct once again was to demur. But the man insisted.

'I'm sure that you must be tired, but we live at the bottom of the hill. And I can help you with your load. My husband and I, our families know what it is to travel. Over a hundred years ago, maybe, but they know. His family fled famine. Mine escaped poverty. They made their lives here working with statuary. They were a little bit like your family, I would guess. Here – if you change your mind.'

The man fished a scrap of paper from out of the breast pocket of his shirt and scribbled down an address.

'Thank you. I would love to join you. But first, I shall rest here for a little. And my offering can stay here.'

'Excellent! We will look forward to your company. See you later!'

Maria smiled and waved the man back down the hill, then returned to her seat against the colossal stone foot. She burned the scrap of paper with the glowing tip of the cigarette, deliberately, systematically, one little hole after another, until it was obliterated. The man would be disappointed when she didn't show up for dinner, she supposed, not realising that she had more important gifts to offer. The details of that particular man were of no consequence and forgotten almost as soon as they were heard; he was merely one of millions. Instead, Maria ran her hand over the smooth stone of the foot and thought of her brother's enigmatic sculptures, the organic forms and flattened planes that spoke of the badlands of their country.

Those badlands had slithered along the coast, usurping the people's claim on the land and the sea and displacing family farms, until they had finally reached Maria's home. The soldiers who arrived in their wake had insisted that Mo create work that reflected their vision of the land. The more ambiguous his work became, the harder they pressed. Eventually, the week before Maria and Mo were to begin their journey, a small group of soldiers came to their door in the night. They took Mo to the gorge in the badlands and chained him to a block of marble, leaving him with no food, no water, no clothes – just a tiny chisel. When the baying crowd arrived at the gorge to dance and drink and celebrate the long-awaited arrival of the torrential seasonal rains, Maria had slipped away under their cover, but she would never forget the leering faces of the soldiers and her fellow citizens who cheered them on.

Maria screwed her eyes tightly shut and shook her head, trying to rid herself of the memory. With eyes closed, she felt like a marble held comfortably in the palm of the natural amphitheatre formed by the hills to the south and west. But the world had stopped, so long ago now, and Maria sat there, stationary, with no use for good luck or bad luck. Each gathered in its own pool and dissipated or did not. It was hardly of any matter any-more. She was the maker of fortune now. After taking a final drag on a second, chain-lit cigarette, Maria ground it violently into the ground, threw the tiny marble at the hills, and opened the small hatch in the colossal foot set in the hollow above the heel.

Immediately, her mood lightened.

'Hello, dear boy,' she said to the smaller, ragged foot inside. Fresh blood glistened where its leg stopped halfway up the calf and the light of the streetlamps snaked into the compartment. Maria winced at the thought of the pile of partially-formed viscera and the fresh and exposed nerve endings that grew from the leg into a shallow pool of syrupy liquid, unconnected and screaming into an inhuman void.

'Our pain is almost over,' she promised.

Maria had been living a half-life since that day in the gorge, a half-life that felt like it had lasted hundreds of millions of years. Now, the people here had given her purpose again, an opportunity to wreak her revenge upon their oppressors – for were not all oppressors one and the same? These people could use her talents, and in return, they had agreed to grant her use of the facilities she needed for her own work. Regenerative medicine was a piece of piss for a world-renowned expert in nuclear science and atomic theory; Maria simply needed the equipment.

As his nervous system and brain stem had started to flicker into this new existence, all that what-had-been-Mo could register was the huge discomfort of phantom limbs – his little, half-formed foot was the least of it. That, and then, eventually, the painful gabbling of the kind man outside hitting his auditory nerve, and the carefully measured words of the woman who knew that, in time, all that would be left of the kind man was a screaming human shadow scorched into stone.

Mo would live again, Maria knew, and while the final yards of his rebirth would be the hardest, their vengeance would be swift and irresistible.

Ricky Monahan Brown was moved to become a writer after he suffered a catastrophic haemorrhagic stroke and realised he had stories to tell about it. *Stroke: A 5% Chance of Survival* went on to become one of *The Scotsman*'s Scottish Books of 2019, and his short fiction has been widely published. Ricky is a regular attendee at the Literary Salon and in 2019 had the huge pleasure of being a guest author discussing memoir-writing together with Catherine Simpson. He enjoys cinema, is working on short and feature film scripts, and is the least musical member of the band Nerd Bait.

Scotland's Colours

Sara Sheridan

Blousy blue,
Bluebell blue,
Brave.
And over the crest
Gorse yellow,
Ridiculous,
'60s neon
And green.
Impenetrable,
Like it was shot
In Technicolour

Light late
Half light,
Then darkness,
A million stars
Clouds like muslin.
The smell of it.
Harder to capture than
Gushing water,
Moss and riverbank,
Mud and rockface.

And in the moonlight,
A slash of flowers:
Blood red,
And no one would believe
The colours of Scotland.
My God. The air so clear.
Miles of silence.
Endless change.
And before us,
A million years
Of art
On the hills.

Sara Sheridan has written more than 20 books and works in both commercial fiction and non-fiction, several of which have made the bestsellers charts. Her work has been shortlisted for the Wilbur Smith, Saltire, and David Hume prizes. She is fascinated by history and its impact on our lives, researching not only in archives but using historical artefacts, art, and the fabric of our built and rural environment. Sara has been a sporadic attendee of the Literary Salon for over a decade. She loves being by the sea, is a voracious reader, and is a campaigner for equality issues (currently supporting the Witches of Scotland campaign).

The Music Man

Ron Butlin

(from a novel in progress)

The platform was crowded, the man could hardly have been any closer and yet, at the very instant he jumped, you saw only what seemed to be a scrap of paper blown in front of the driver's cab.

It was a Wednesday morning and you were about to begin another day as an executive biscuit-man at Majestics. Before jumping, the man had asked you the time. '8:21,' you told him and joked about your biscuit week being nearly half-eaten. The last person he saw was you; the last voice he heard was yours. Seconds later, the man's day, his week and his whole life came to an abrupt halt. More than thirty years on, you are still carrying that abruptness inside you like a hidden fracture, a wound that might burst open at any moment.

*

SATURDAY

It is well after midnight when Morris begins his descent into the village. With only a sliver of moon and a handful of stars above, it feels like he's coming in to land on an unknown planet.

Pulling up near the cottage, he cuts the engine, kills the headlights and starts to breathe again. Two hours driving at night is two hours too many and he sits for a moment to gather himself. The cottages on either side are in darkness, their doors shut, their curtains pulled. As if it had been marked with an X, he seems to have parked on the very spot where he had seen his father for the last time, standing and shaking his fist at him. Pure coincidence, of course. For a moment, though, Morris feels tempted to run the car back and forth over the ground, grinding that particular memory into the dirt. But he doesn't. Getting old is his last chance to let go of the bad stuff.

Too cold for hanging around, taking trips down memory lane. He grabs his coat and holdall from the rear seat, zap-locks the car, and scrunches up to the garden gate. Same as all those years ago, it gives an unoiled screech. An owl screeches back to tell him he's not alone.

He follows the path round to the cottage entrance. As a small boy he boasted that he lived in the only back-to-front house in the whole of Scotland. With its stretch of blank wall bordering the road and its entrance and windows looking out onto the garden at the rear, it is a cottage that long ago turned its back on the world.

Once inside, Morris fumbles for a light switch, snapping it on and off several times before he remembers – no electricity. No torch either, he forgot to bring one. Pitch-dark, and even colder inside than out. Maybe coming back here wasn't such a great idea? Not a helpful thought.

By the light from his mobile he can see it's his mother's old kitchen. Or was. No cooker anymore, no fridge, no cupboards, the remains of a wrecked sink unit, a bucket with a hole in it, broken slates lying everywhere. The bare walls are a Jackson Pollock of mould and damp stains, and the floor shows more cement than linoleum.

The fusebox used to be on the wall next to the back door... and it still is. Ms Estate Agent told him the electricity had been disconnected at source. Morris flicks the red switch to ON to check and, sure enough, nothing happens. Which is a problem he can work around. He hopes. He has brought the pliers and magnet, but, with his phone battery down to 8%, he'll need to move fast.

She mentioned... something... the something. *The sink unit*. She had mentioned a drawer in what's left of the sink unit. Where there might be....

Where there *is*. A candle. Matches. Thank fuck. Only a stump, but it should last long enough.

Luckily the electricity meter is nearly as ancient as he is. He flicks the fusebox switch a second time. Still nothing. And so, as Jacko showed him all those years ago back in Middle Earth, he tracks the wires connecting the meter to the outside mains supply. Things are looking good and, as a bonus, the candle seems a slow burner. Pausing only to stamp his feet every few minutes and blow on his fingers to warm them, he gets on with the snipping and splicing. Ten minutes later, he has snipped what needs snipped, spliced what needs spliced, and bypassed what needs bypassed. Far too many wires, of course, but he has dealt with the right ones. He thinks. It's been a long time.

When he flicks the switch again, it is third time lucky. The kitchen light snaps on and a reassuring hum comes from the electricity meter. He slaps on the magnet. Job done.

Next up, the water.

On with both taps at once. Not a fucking drop. Either the water's been turned off, or else the pipes froze a while back and are still frozen. He'll go with *turned off*. The second option doesn't bear thinking about.

The stopcock is under the sink. After a couple of dry coughs, out come a few rusty-looking gushes which soon begin running clear. Thank fuck.

Before hypothermia sets in, he unpacks his camping stove and small saucepan, and puts some water on for tea. Which will give him time to check out what's left of the house where he was born. A moment later he is back for the stump of candle.

It turns out there's not much to see. His childhood bedroom, just off the kitchen, has most of its ceiling lying on the floor. There is no light bulb in his parents' old room at the other end of the cottage. By candlelight, the large hole in the floor suggests the luxury of a sunken bath, minus the bath and the luxury. No light bulb in the bathroom either, and one glance in the door is enough. Which leaves only the sitting room. He'll sleep there.

In the kitchen, the water is coming to the boil and the phone has died. After giving the draining board a wipe to clear away the dead flies, creepy-crawlies and mouse shit, he unpacks his goodybag of food grabbed at the last minute before rushing out his flat: two tins of ravioli, tin of peas, tin of Scotch Broth, tin of frankfurters; half a packet of Coco Pops, an individual pork pie, a couple of bananas, some bread, butter, ginger snaps, teabags, packet of rice, pickled onions. He forgot to bring salt and he can picture the carton of milk still sitting on its shelf in the fridge. At the very bottom of the bag he finds the no-wine and no-brandy he packed at the last minute.

From now on, every day is the first day. He switches off the camping stove and reaches for—

No mug. He forgot that as well.

Quick peer under the sink. More dead flies, spider-webs, assorted junk, jumble sale crockery, and a pile of old rags that might once have been tea-towels. Mouse shit everywhere like a topping of hundreds and thou-sands. Then… no handle, but it'll do.

A swirl-out under the tap, and in with the teabag. A bent spoon from under the sink gets a quick rinse, then he stirs, fishes out the teabag and, not a moment too soon, clasps his hands round the mug for warmth. The pork pie is gone in seconds.

Mobile plugged in, he has a few ginger snaps for des-sert, followed by a banana.

Ping, ping, ping, ping. A rush of texts from son Tom and daughter Elise, known affectionately as The Accusations.

Arrived okay, Dad? Are you okay, Dad? Call me. Call me. Dad? Let's hear from you! Pleeeeeease.

He had upped and left Edinburgh without giving notice, texted them last thing as he was going out the door of his flat. Elise had called back immediately. She told him she was shocked that he'd not phoned to talk things through with them first. He apologised to her, then stepped back indoors and phoned Tom to apolo-gise to him as well. Then came the three-way discussion, extra-complicated as his phone is too old to do con-ference calls. They texted him their comments, and he responded by phoning each of them back in turn. He felt like he was Beethoven using his conversation books once the great composer had gone stone deaf. The Accusations were excited about his commission, but kept on about a possible lockdown because of the virus and how he might get trapped away from home and not be able to get back. *No problem*, was his quick reply. Lockdown would give him all the peace and quiet he'd need to work on his quartet. Meanwhile, it was getting later and later and he kept picturing end-of-winter icy roads and snow in the Moffat Hills. Finally it was settled that he'd text them last thing every night to let them know he was fine. No other contact, except in an emergency. That was the agreement. But shivering in his coat in this unheated kitchen he is pleased they have violated protocol, pleased almost to the point of tears. He knows he should count himself lucky. Correction: he *does*. His children really care.

Fuck. Because, like a bad taste that he has not got the courage to spit out, here comes the real question: Tom and Elise care, but does *he*? They are anxious to know if their dad's all right. Well, is he? He starts to text back: **Thanks, Tom, Thanks, Elise. All's well. I'm fine. Everything's fine....**

Another unhelpful thought: Planning to stay alone in a derelict cottage where he could freeze to death near enough – and their seventy-year-old dad thinks he is *fine*? Really? He takes a deep breath, then carries on: **Getting myself settled in now and off to bed soon. Thanks for all your texts. Please don't worry. Sleep well. Night-night!**

Adding a triple thumbs-up, a heart, a few XXXs, and signing off: *Love you, Dad*. Because he does. Of course he does. Loving *them* is not the problem. He taps *Send*.

Starting to feel really tired he slips outside for an *al fresco* pee and a glance up at more stars than he has seen in years. Living in the city he has forgotten what a glorious sight they are. When he starts to count them, the more he counts the more there are, which feels strangely reassuring. Quick shake off, and back indoors. Light a fire, or go straight to bed and leave the rest of the mod-cons till daylight? No contest. The torn cement sacks, broken bricks, rubble, and lumps of rock-hard plaster tossed into a corner, he unrolls his sleeping bag along the back wall. His holdall will do as a pillow. *The clartier the cosier*, as he used to say when he was a kid. Ms Estate Agent would be shocked. He can still hear the bewilderment in her voice. *There's no furniture, are you going to sleep on the floor?*

As there is no bulb in the light fixture and the one in the kitchen is too high up to reach, he melts the candle stump at its base and sticks it onto a lump of brick to make a cosy-looking bedlamp. Shoes kicked off, he sets a new record for sliding fully dressed into a sleeping bag, and pulls his coat on top for a quilt. Candle snuffed out with a wet thumb, he closes his eyes. And... gradually, ever so gradually, starts to warm up.

A non-stop *drip-splat, drip-splat, drip drip drip...* comes through the wall from the bathroom. A leak, but it doesn't sound like a big one. Its steady rhythm is reassuring, comforting almost. He'll deal with it tomorrow. A final thought before drifting off to sleep, a good one this time: Returning here after circumnavigating his threescore and ten, he really has come full circle. This time he will get things right.

Ron Butlin is an international prize-winning novelist, and former Edinburgh Makar / Poet Laureate. His work has been translated into over a dozen languages. Before becoming a full-time writer he was a footman, a barnacle scraper on Thames barges, a song-lyricist, and a male model. He attended the very first Edinburgh Literary Salon over ten years ago and still enjoys going there to meet friends and gossip. *The Music Man*, a work in progress, is the sequel to his acclaimed novel *The Sound of My Voice*.

Hockey *ke Jaadugar*

Srishti Chaudhary

'Just act like it's any other day,' Pooja said.

Shannu gave her a meaningful sideways glance, his light brown eyes seeming darker than usual. 'It *is* any other day.'

'Don't overdo it with the hockey stick though, like you always do,' she told him, letting out a little giggle, looking down at their sad excuses for hockey sticks. 'Everyone on the street knows you're not any good.'

'I will be one day. Hockey *ka jaadugar*,' Shannu said, staring dreamily into the distance. The *Wizard of Hockey*. 'Major Dhyan Chand Singh.'

Shannu had the lightest hair. People said it made him look like one of the white people, and he wasn't sure whether to be proud or disgusted.

'Also, don't run too fast, or they might not notice us,' Pooja told him.

'I know.'

'And don't do your stupid dance if you score a goal, please; we don't want to scare people.'

'If they aren't scared by your face, I think they'll be fine with my dance,' Shannu said.

'Oh, ha ha.... '

They stood in silence for a minute until they finally heard the sound of the cuckoo: the signal from Ferozeji. Pooja's eyes were hard-set and Shannu's jaw tightened. They looked towards each other, resolute.

'Ready,' Pooja said, more an answer than a question.

Shannu nodded. 'Let's go.'

The course of Indian independence then, that warm February afternoon, depended on one little boy and one little girl.

The recently christened Bentinck Circle was like a wreath, with sprawling Amaltas trees running along its circumference; come spring, those trees would bathe the roads in a shower of yellow. In the centre of the circle stood a Union Jack – red, white, and blue, caressed by the light breeze – surrounded by an eight-foot-tall opaque fence. The scent of *jalebis* and *aloo kachori* cut through the air, and the sound of their sizzling in the background was punctuated by the rattle of the *tongas* and the cluck of the horses' hooves. Further on in the circle, the marketplace began, where hawkers spread out fruits and vegetables in baskets, ready for sale. Earthen pots and mugs sat balanced atop each other, next to the little boy who would polish the leather shoes of the white people when they passed by, his arm resting on the shoeshine kit.

As the road curved further on at Bentinck Circle, there was a row of low-rise buildings: shops on the ground level advertised with colourful boards, Dewan Watch Co. being the largest and most prominent of them all. The offices of lawyers and accountants – the only ones who could afford the rent – occupied the first level, and above those were the lawyers' and accountants' houses. Beneath, where the street turned, near to the path that led out of the circle, stood two British guards: Yellow Hair and Brown Hair, as Pooja and Shannu called them.

Yellow Hair was very tall and very white, with striking blue eyes that contrasted sharply with the khaki uniform he wore. He kept his shirt smartly tucked, with his trousers held up by a dark brown belt and his boots shining.

Brown Hair had a nest of curls on his head, light freckles on his face, and short, stubby fingers. The golden buttons on his blazer glinted under the Indian sun, as he fidgeted with them constantly. He looked around with a curled lip and a disdainful glare.

They both stood under the shade of the Amaltas trees with their chests puffed out, maintaining a severe demeanour for the people who passed by: the women with their heads covered by cotton drapes and the men in their white *dhotis* and Gandhi *topis*.

'Children, this depends on you now,' Feroze*ji* had told them. 'Each of us have a part to play in this struggle. This is your part.'

Pooja and Shannu had nodded, with all the seriousness of nine-year-olds. It had already been impressed upon them that their task was an important one; Feroze*ji* had made sure of that.

'*Bapu* requires the utmost support from all of us right now. All of us, no matter where we live. In two weeks, he will begin the march and it will be like nothing the world has ever seen before. But for it to be a success, he needs people to stand by him and support him, to walk with him. He needs people from here, from *Dilli*. It cannot be done without the people here.'

'We are with him, Feroze*ji*,' Shannu had said, and as he nodded his head, there was fire in his eyes.

'Yes, Feroze*ji*.' Pooja had nodded as well, determined not to be left behind.

Feroze*ji* had put a hand on Shannu's shoulder and smiled at Pooja. 'Then we have to make sure that we are able to deliver this material out from the press. You know that the press is illegal. Of course, Shyam*ji* at Dewan Watch knows that we are using his upstairs office to run it, but he told us that we have to manage sneaking these out on our own. Especially with this quantity.... '

Pooja and Shannu had listened with rapt attention; they knew their time had come. Their parents worked all day for the struggle and were frequently jailed; Pooja and Shannu were their legacy.

'But Feroze*ji*,' Pooja had asked, 'what is written on it?'

'Propaganda,' he'd said. 'Posters, leaflets, news.... They will go up all over the city. The more they tear down, the more we will put up.'

She'd nodded quickly, eager to prove she'd understood. Her mother had told her: *there is nothing bigger than the country*.

'Tell me the plan again,' Feroze*ji* said.

'We will play hockey and distract them, the two officers,' Shannu began. 'We'll fight over the rules, and then we'll ask them to show us how to play.'

'If they say no to that,' Pooja added, 'we'll go back to the spot and start fighting, create a big drama, so they'll be distracted and move away from the tram path.'

'The point is to take them away from there, because it's the only exit from the circle.'

'And once they come with you to the goalpost?' Feroze*ji* asked.

'You'll be watching us from the windows,' Pooja

recited. 'We have to keep them there till there's another cuckoo's call. That would mean you have been able to exit by the path.'

Ferozeji stared at them for a few seconds. '*Jai Hind*,' he finally said. 'Victory to India.'

Unlike the other circles in Delhi, Bentinck Circle had just one road in and out. Usually, this path became congested towards the evening, especially since it had been included on the tram route and a track had been carved out. It was this path that they needed to arrange for Ferozeji, the path that Yellow Hair and Brown Hair guarded. There had been intelligence about low-key nationalist activities taking place in Bentinck Circle ahead of a planned march, but no specifics about when, where, or how, and so the two officers had just recently been stationed there to keep an eye on the general goings-on of the street. Days had passed without anything seeming out of place. The officers might have taken it as merely a preventive measure; all the action was taking place down south, after all, in Gujarat, at the heels of Gandhi.

Pooja and Shannu stood a little way away from the two soldiers and began their game, clumsily crashing their sticks together, jamming them on the ball, making a lot more noise than necessary. Pooja clashed her stick against Shannu's with unbridled vigour, and she had a steadfast look when he grinned up at her.

'Focus,' she told him, making a jab, and he almost laughed aloud.

They were now behind the officers, and Pooja tried to retrieve the ball from Shannu, aggressively hitting his stick instead, drawing more and more attention to themselves. They cursed each other, growing louder by the minute, but they both saw, from the corner of their eyes, Brown Hair glaring at them.

Pooja took her cue from Shannu's surreptitious nod and yelled even louder, 'Take that, you bastard!' and almost made Shannu trip. Shannu took the opportunity and pushed Pooja on the shoulder, making her lose her balance, so that Brown Hair was finally compelled to interfere.

'Hey, you two!' Brown Hair yelled. 'What are you doing?'

Pooja and Shannu looked towards him, surprised and subdued, dropping their hockey sticks and bowing, folding their hands on their fronts.

'Come here!' Brown Hair yelled.

Pooja jumped, glancing at Shannu, but they both walked forward, eyes facing the ground.

'What do you think you're doing?' Brown Hair said sternly, as Yellow Hair glared.

'We were trying to play hockey, *sahib*,' Shannu said in a small voice.

'He pushed me, *sahib*,' Pooja said. 'It is a foul.'

'She was cheating the whole time, *sahib*!'

'Keep quiet,' Yellow Hair said. He glanced at Brown Hair and both of them looked Pooja and Shannu up and down.

'What were you playing?' Brown Hair asked.

'Hockey, *sahib*,' Shannu replied, 'You know Hockey *ka jaadugar*? Major Dhyan Chand Singh?'

They looked at Shannu quietly; of course they had heard of him.

'You want to play hockey like Major Dhyan Chand?' Yellow Hair fumbled the name with his British accent.

Pooja and Shannu nodded excitedly.

'Who gave you these sticks?' Brown Hair asked them.

'I got these, *sahib*,' Pooja said quickly, her braids bouncing. 'They are my brother's old sticks.'

They stared at Pooja for long, quiet moment. Shannu, noticing this, interrupted, 'Can you teach us, *sahib*? You must know real hockey.'

'You shouldn't play hockey like this, on this street,' Yellow Hair dismissed. 'It's a complicated game and requires proper training.'

'Please, *sahib*,' Shannu said, looking up at them in deference. 'Just for a few minutes, *sahib*. It will be like a dream for us.'

After a few seconds, Brown Hair looked at Yellow Hair. 'What do you think, Tom? Fancy shooting a few?'

Yellow Hair looked sceptical at first, but then shrugged. 'Alright.'

'We have made a goalpost there, *sahib*,' Shannu said, pointing in the opposite direction, away from the path of the tram. 'We can go there.'

The officers put their hands out for the sticks, and both Shannu and Pooja eagerly handed them over, leading the officers to their makeshift goalposts in the Bentinck Circle. Once the officers were engaged in the game for a few minutes, Feroze*ji* would have enough time to sneak out from the other side of the circle, along with two other men, and exit from the path where the tram cut across.

'Look, we made these ourselves, *sahib*,' Pooja said.

The soldiers looked a little uncomfortable being addressed so freely by a little Indian girl, but went with her anyway.

'Do you play a lot of hockey, *sahib*?' Shannu asked, to keep the conversation going.

'Quite a bit, yes,' Yellow Hair mused.

'I was pretty good,' Brown Hair said. 'I once played in a tournament in Warwickshire for my university; scored three goals in the final match, practically led them to victory.'

'Is that so?' Yellow Hair said wryly. 'Where's the ball, then?'

'Here, *sahib*,' Shannu said, handing it to him. 'Can I be the goalkeeper, *sahib*?'

Yellow Hair nodded, and Pooja obediently took her place behind the goalpost where she could catch the ball if it escaped, and where she also had a good view of the end of the street, to make sure that Feroze*ji* would not be seen. Yellow Hair and Brown Hair passed the ball between them a few times and Shannu asked them, '*Sahib*, what position do you play?'

'I was always the attacker,' Brown Hair replied, more to Yellow Hair than to Shannu.

'Curious,' Yellow Hair said, 'I don't see a lot of attacking here.'

'Wait for it.'

After exchanging a few words, both of them decided to take turns at shooting. Brown Hair went first. Pooja, stationed behind the goalpost, jumped and waved her arms constantly, so as to draw attention to herself, just in case Feroze*ji* was somewhere in the vicinity: he'd see them there and keep away. Shannu repeatedly moved between the left and the right goalpost but let almost every goal in, his hockey stick useless in his hands.

'I told you he's bad, *sahib*,' Pooja said meaningfully, when she noticed a hint of impatience on their faces, 'and he wants to be like Hockey *ka jaadugar!*'

'Major Dhyan Chand Singh, eh?' Yellow Hair asked. 'Have you seen him play?'

'Yes, *sahib*, once, but from very far away,' Shannu replied.

Yellow Hair stared at Pooja for some time, unsure of what to make of her. 'It's surprising to see you play here, little girl. I mean, I haven't seen that many girls—'

'I tell her the same thing, *sahib*,' Shannu said, 'but she follows me everywhere.'

Pooja told him to shut his mouth, and then went on to narrate a long-winded story about how she had saved *annas* for a few months and then exchanged them with her brother for the hockey sticks. 'My brother needed the money, because he likes a girl in secret, and he wanted to save money so he can marry her.' At the back of her mind, she counted how many minutes they had been there; but she had learnt the story so well that she could narrate it flawlessly. She explained how her brother had been a bit suspicious over why she'd wanted the hockey sticks, because he'd thought that she wanted them to gift them to Shannu.

'Can you believe it, *sahib*?!' she asked, snorting.

Brown Hair handed the hockey stick to Yellow Hair, who took it with contrition. He couldn't believe that this little girl was narrating her entire life story to him as if he were her best friend. He made his face a little sterner and looked straight ahead. After a few seconds, he asked them, despite himself, 'What is your caste?'

Suddenly standing to attention, Shannu said, 'My father's a trader, *sahib*. He brings silk from down south, and sells it here. He has the best silk saris in the district.'

'Mine too, *sahib*,' Pooja said. 'He has a shop of cashews and nuts.'

'A *shop* is a big word for it, don't you think?' Shannu asked Pooja, who made a mocking face in response.

Yellow Hair shot the ball a few times, and Shannu couldn't stop a single goal. Yellow Hair gave Brown Hair a look, which he picked up.

'Right, I'm going to guard the goalpost now,' he said. For Shannu and Pooja it couldn't get better, for that meant both officers were completely engaged and distracted from everything else. Pooja and Shannu stood as spectators, giving a cheer now and then to keep the spirit up; the sight must have seemed so strange that a few bystanders began to gather on the other side of the street, watching them curiously. A few men had stopped their bicycles and now stood watching the two British officers playing hockey with two little Indian children.

Finally, a cuckoo called, and Shannu cast a quick glance at Pooja. She gave him the briefest of nods and he got ready to run to the other side of the circle to check if everything really was clear, and that Ferozeji had gone on to the path with the propaganda.

Suddenly, he gave Pooja a shove. She lost her balance and almost fell to the ground, as he ran off to the side of the printing press, laughing and acting as if they'd had a little fight. The officers didn't seem to notice him at first, their eyes concentrated on the goal post, but looked up as he disappeared around the curve of the street.

Shannu ran across the circle, dashing inside the printing press over Dewan Watch Co., asking with impertinence if Ferozeji had left, to which they replied in the affirmative. He then ran further along Bentinck Circle, going around the Union Jack, past the *tongas* and the marketplace, the vegetables in the baskets and the earthen pots on display, and the little boy with the shoe polish. He passed the *aloo kachori* and *jalebi* stands, his stomach grumbling. He looked about wildly to see if anything was amiss when he spotted Ferozeji's back at the end of the path, as the tram came by and blocked him completely from the view.

In wild haste, Shannu ran up further, for Pooja was still with the officers. He had pushed her rather hard; he couldn't wait to tell her that they had managed it. It was the third job the struggle had required of them. Shannu's great wish in life was to be arrested and jailed like Bhagat Singh, and Pooja had said that he was stupid to think that because being in jail would mean he couldn't do any useful work. But he could already imagine the pride on his father's face for distracting Yellow Hair and Brown Hair. He ran in headiness, imagining the Union Jack replaced by the Indian flag, Gandhi's great *charkha*, flying in the centre of Bentinck Circle. He ran so fast that he crashed right into Yellow Hair, and fell backwards from the impact.

In one swift motion, Yellow Hair had Shannu pinned to the ground, holding him by his collar, his eyes cold blue and hateful now. Shannu's own smaller ones looked back defiantly, trying to hide his fear. The grip around his collar tightened, and Yellow Hair went on staring at him without blinking, his gaze scanning every inch of his face, from his light brown hair which had streaks of black, his button eyes, the creased skin on his forehead. Shannu's mouth parted slightly, his lips going dry.

Yellow Hair bared his teeth, clutching Shannu's collar even tighter, and he hissed in a voice so quiet that Shannu was surprised he could hear it. 'What have you done?'

Pooja rounded the corner, but stopped, staring in terror at Shannu's wide eyes, Yellow Hair holding him tightly by the throat. A shiver ran through her.

'What's going on, Tom?' Brown Hair asked urgently, coming to a halt beside her.

Pooja looked about wildly, her mind racing and her heart pumping faster and faster. Her nostrils flared, and she took an instinctive step away from Brown Hair. Pooja didn't want this. She didn't like jail.

Shannu refused to meet her eyes, for Yellow Hair still watched him without a blink.

Pooja's throat went dry as she thought of Ferozeji, far and away. She thought of the posters that were out, that would line the walls of the city in a few hours. She thought of Gandhi marching towards Dandi, and the millions that would follow him, the millions that would make up India. Their own India; their separate India. She thought of herself and Shannu in that India, one that would be just for them. She thought of her mother fasting in jail, and she thought of Shannu in a flash.

'Take him to jail, *sahib*!' she yelled at the top of her voice; it rose above the *tongas* and the increasing chatter on Bentinck Circle, as people slowly began to crowd around them. Yellow Hair looked back at her, startled by her shout, his grip on Shannu's collar loosening.

'Take him, *sahib*, take him! He deserves it. He's always hitting me. He thinks he is a revolutionary! He wants to be like Bhagat Singh; he wants everyone to admire him.'

Yellow Hair breathed heavily, as Brown Hair looked at him for orders. When none were given, Brown Hair turned to Pooja and told her to keep quiet.

'He says he wants to die for the country, *sahib*,' Pooja told the whole street, as someone whistled from among the crowd. 'He says he *really* wants to die.'

Brown Hair immediately charged towards her and

grabbed her by the neck. Pooja screamed. There were angry murmurs in the crowd.

'Release her,' said Yellow Hair.

Brown Hair hesitated, but eventually let go of Pooja's throat, and she gasped.

Yellow Hair pushed Shannu down on the ground, giving him a menacing look. 'If I ever see you on this street again,' he said in a voice that rang above all others, a voice that matched the gun he held at his belt, 'if I ever see *either* of you on this street, I will personally take you to jail. A jail in England.'

Shannu pursed his lips and Pooja looked indignant.

'Get out of here,' he said.

Shannu got up, wiping every bit of dust from his clothes and buttoning up his collar. Pooja started to follow him, but then came back and held out her hands to Brown Hair for her hockey sticks; he looked at her malevolently and handed them to her.

She said a quiet, 'Sorry, *sahib*,' and walked away from Bentinck Circle, trailing Shannu, barely able to contain her smile.

Hockey *ke jaadugar*, she told herself. Pooja and Shannu: *The Wizards of Hockey*.

Srishti Chaudhary is the author of *Lallan Sweets* and *Once upon a Curfew*, both published by Penguin Random House India. She studied Creative Writing at the University of Edinburgh. For her, there's no city in the world like Edinburgh. She's currently a research scholar at the University of Tübingen in Germany, and is working on her third novel. She likes long walks and good conversation, even better when together.

Found

PENNY HODSON

Cold Tea

Jen McGregor

It's cold. It's wet. The moon's malingering behind a cloud. Midsummer's Eve my arse. There's no Summer to be Mid.

My cagoule is leaking. I've given up on keeping dry. I've got a flask of lukewarm tea though, so that's something. It's 23:50. Only ten minutes to go. Not that anything's going to happen.

I'm so well prepared though. Digital camera, analogue, night vision, full spectrum, you name it. Magnetic-field-measuring-thing. I called in so many favours to get my hands on all this. Seemed like such a good idea at the...

Well, actually it seemed like a stupid idea. I just need to make something that people will notice, before I reach complete destitution. Even if it's some stupid Real Banshees of North Lanarkshire type of—

Shit! Shit shit shit! What is that? What—

Oh. My phone. Hahaha. Should've put it on silent. Let's see... Ugh. A string of emojis, little sheet-ghosts. My friends are nothing if not supportive.

Midnight! I check my equipment. Everything's doing what it's – Wait, no it's not. There's a flashing light, why's there a flashing light? No no no, don't do this to me, I need you, I need you for this to look even slightly—

'Art thou all right?'

What? I'm losing the plot, my mind's playing tricks, I thought I heard—

'Art thou all right?'

That... That's...

That thing in front of me, misty and swirling and... Tudor? That's a French hood, it's got the shape and... seriously, French hoods? A ghost, a fucking ghost, and the first thing I notice is clothes? What is wrong with me?

'Be not afraid. I, Lady Kathryn de Courcy, shalt do thee no harm! I mourn the loss of my beloved – oh Henry, Henry!'

'Henry?'

'We were star-crossed!' She's pulling a semi-transparent handkerchief from semi-transparent cleavage. 'He fell from his horse in the woods, and 'twas I who nursed him back to health! Alas, that a simple nun should capture a king's heart!'

A king? A nun? A king? This is a ghost, this is an actual ghost, there's no such thing but this is an actual – 'A king?!'

'Yes! Hadst I not been promised to Christ, I would hadst been his queen, not that adulteress Catherine Howard! Alack!'

An actual ghost. Telling me its actual story. 'What happened?'

'I, in despair, brewed a tisane of nightshade and hemlock, and now I walk the earth, doomed.... '

She's still talking, the actual ghost, but there's something.... I don't know what it is, but something's not quite... Never mind. 'Wow. What a time to be alive! The dissolution of the monasteries!'

'Quite so! And he would fain have done the nunneries too, but for my pleading!'

'My God, that's... Wait, though. Nuns were affected too, weren't they? I thought they were. Nunneries burned and everything.'

'... Not that I know of.'

'I was sure they... Hang on, who did you say he married?'

'Er... the adulteress Catherine Howard?'

'But... Look, I'm not trying to be difficult here, but wasn't the dissolution like, twenty years earlier? In Anne Boleyn's time?'

'I was... sheltered! How was an innocent maid to know anything about these great matters?'

'You'd know about the burning of nunneries if you were a nun, though. All this massive social change going on and you—'

'All right! Fine! You win! I'm not a Tudor lady, I didn't have an affair with Henry VIII, I'm not Kathryn de Courcy. My name's Kate Kershaw and I'm from Cumber-bloody-nauld, okay? Happy now?'

'I'm sorry. It's just... why? The Tudor thing, I mean. You're a ghost pretending to be a different ghost?'

'Didn't want to spend all eternity as Kate bloody Kershaw, did I? What's the point in being the ghost of someone boring?'

'You're a ghost. That's not boring.'

'What's exciting about dying in 1986? Of a bloody asthma attack!'

'You get to be a ghost for an asthma attack?'

'I know! I thought ghosts were all people who died

romantic deaths full of unfulfilled longing. But they're not. They're just people like me... Stupid.'

'No, no. I get it. I really do. I really do.... '

'There's this one girl, Hetty, down at Hampton Court,' Kate's in full flow now. She hasn't had anyone to talk to for a while. 'She was a tea lady in the 1840s. Fell down the stairs, broke her neck, now she's Catherine Howard! Runs screaming down the Long Gallery. She loves it. Didn't fancy that myself. I wanted to make up my own story.'

'Understandable. Might be better to steer clear of specific details in future though. Or haunt a library, do some research.'

The viewscreen on my camera lights up. The old school camera starts winding itself on. The ghost glances at them.

'Oh, those should be fine now,' she says. 'They come back on eventually. After people have run away.'

I check the footage. Disappointing. Nothing I couldn't have faked. I switch back to shooting mode, and she's there! Semi-transparent but visible! Ha! Amazing!

I show her the images. She preens – she's never seen herself in full regalia. She insists I take more pictures. I oblige. Formal portrait. Candid. Prostrate with pretend grief.

As I click and click, I feel the camera turning to gold in my hands. What if Kate got her story straight? What if some intrepid soul did some research, found the right dates, made her story plausible? The true, authentic, accurate life story of Lady Kathryn de Courcy is starting to take shape in my head... Most people will assume it's fake, which it will be, but if anyone learns the truth, well... even better!

I direct the ghost to pose on her knees, head flung back, bewailing the loss of her love. This, I know, will be the cover of my bestseller. The picture in the history books.

A drop of water wends its way down the back of my neck. This time I barely notice it at all.

Jen McGregor is a playwright and director whose recent credits include *Vox* (Charioteer Theatre / Piccolo Theatre of Milan) and *Heaven Burns* (previously Scotland's History Festival). Her short play, *Love Love*, the story of a dangerously lovelorn SatNav, was published in *New Writing Scotland 34* in August 2016.

Louvain Epiphany

Seán Martin

In his *Portrait of a Man*,
Dieric Bouts did not elaborate much
behind his nameless sitter.

Just a muddy wash of wall,
the casement framing woods
and a town stilled in early mist.

Someone there has spoken his name
and he has somehow heard.
But a detail snags the eye:

1462 is clawed into the wall,
mason's mark or pilgrim sign.
Bouts looked back, balanced

on the cusp of that room,
its morning and its silence,
birds looping round towers,

a clatter of ropes at the well.
Shutters came off as stoves lit up,
a day's work waking.

All the while, Bouts' sitter
chapel-quiet, cleric's garb newly laundered,
eyes far-seeing.

Bouts knew then what he'd painted.
He finished the town through the window
and graffitied the date

in place of signing his name.

Seán Martin is a writer based in Edinburgh. He won the Wigtown Poetry Prize in 2011, and his first collection of poems is *The Girl Who Got onto the Ferry in Citizen Kane* (Templar Poetry, 2018). His other books include *The Knights Templar: The History & Myths of the Legendary Military Order, The Gnostics: The First Christian Heretics*, and *Andrei Tarkovsky.* Seán has been a regular at the Edinburgh Literary Salon since 2009. He also makes documentaries and holds a PhD in filmmaking.

Weather

Sara Sheridan

In the carwash she tucked us in the back.
After that I was never scared of storms.
Jets and brushes,
clicking slates,
water rushes,
rattling windows,
gushing gutters,
and we drove through.

A lesson.

The nature of weather
and passion.
The way of a broken heart,
a bad day,
a difficult night,
cannot last.

So baby, let me teach you
about weather.
Its sound and confusion,
drama and glory,
rain or wind,
love or loss.
Whatever comes,
never fear
to buckle up
and just drive through.

Sara Sheridan has written more than twenty books and works in both commercial fiction and non-fiction, several of which have made the bestsellers charts. Her work has been shortlisted for the Wilbur Smith, Saltire, and David Hume prizes. She is fascinated by history and its impact on our lives, researching not only in archives but using historical artefacts, art, and the fabric of our built and rural environment. Sara has been a sporadic attendee of the Literary Salon for over a decade. She loves being by the sea, is a voracious reader, and is a campaigner for equality issues (currently supporting the Witches of Scotland campaign).

A Modern Lady's Guide to Beast Hunting

Andrew Jamieson

My Great Aunt Elspeth MacBurram was due to get out of hospital tomorrow, or the day after. She was an enigma in our family. We had travelled up to Edinburgh on the request of the family lawyer, a well-spoken man called Leonid Scarpesian.

Elspeth lived alone in a large Georgian-era townhouse along one of the epic crescents in Edinburgh's New Town. My dad had grown up here. When his father (Elspeth's brother), Hector MacBurram, had disappeared in mysterious circumstances the February before the millennium, Elspeth had become the live-in caretaker for the family home, with my dad's blessing.

Elspeth had been attacked in the house, so Mr Scarpesian had told us. She was suffering from a mild concussion and had light bruising on her face and wrists. She was weak and confused but otherwise seemed fine, Scarpesian reported. She was due to get out of hospital within days, if her progress continued.

'She always was a tough antique,' my dad said.

My mum rolled her eyes. 'Really, Alec.'

My dad never spoke much about his family but announced that we were going to visit Elspeth to see what we could do to help, and that we would be staying at the family home.

He didn't expect my sister and I to come on the trip but I was intrigued, having only visited Edinburgh as a child. I had a clouded recollection of imposing gothic architecture, wide open green spaces, hilly streets, and lots of rain. And we all wanted to know why Elspeth had been attacked. Scarpesian said the police were looking into it.

We travelled by train. None of us spoke much. My dad seemed preoccupied, leaving my mum to fill the void with card games and crossword puzzles. My sister, Jess, won every card game but couldn't stand the crosswords. She'd always been the more competitive daughter.

Staring out the window as we crossed the border into Scotland, I gazed out over rolling hills and shrouded mountain peaks in the distance. Grey skies released their downpour as I imagined giants and trolls battling over land and riches. I drifted off to sleep and when I awoke we were in Edinburgh. I'd had a foggy dream, something to do with walking underneath bridges, looking for lost things. I told Jess about this dream later before bed and she shrugged. 'Dreams aren't an accident,' she said, in that know-it-all manner that annoyed me more than it didn't.

It was late afternoon and it was raining. The clouded skies over Edinburgh were a bruised medley of blues and purples. We got a taxi to Elspeth's home, a tall and narrow, very attractive, old house sandwiched between other similar buildings. The crescent wound along neat, cobbled streets that glistened as we got out of the taxi. My dad had keys, mailed to him by Scarpesian, and after some fiddling with the lock, we entered the house. A hallway greeted us, and a stale smell of dried herbs and damp hit my nose. A shaft of light pierced the gloom and I craned my neck upwards and saw a skylight, streaked with grime, the drab clouds just visible. I noticed that there were three floors with a grand staircase snaking upwards that linked them.

The look on my dad's face, as we walked down the hallway towards the kitchen, was that of a man at once caught in the past, present, and future. He blinked, saw me staring and smiled it away.

'I'll get us some hot drinks,' said Mum. 'Why don't you refamiliarise yourself with the place?' she said to my dad, putting a hand on his left shoulder. He nodded and walked back to the staircase. My sister and I instinctively followed him whilst my mum found the main hall light switches and flicked them on, the shadows fleeing to their corners.

We ascended, following my dad, and reached the first floor. We all looked around, getting our bearings. There were four doors and all were open.

My dad hesitantly walked towards the nearest and peered in. He looked over at us. 'Nothing unusual.'

'Which is Elspeth's room?' Jess asked. 'Is it on this floor?'

My dad shrugged. 'I don't know,' he said. 'I'll finish looking around on this floor, why don't you two head upstairs?'

We obliged, my sister heading to the third floor.

The second floor was much like the first. Four doors, all open. That seemed odd to me. I peered into them all: two were empty, and one was a sitting room, with a sofa, table, and a chest of drawers with all the drawers open; again, odd.

The last room looked to be a study, a desk by the window overlooking the street and bookcases lining the walls. I immediately noticed books on the floor, some spread open, the drawers in the desk open, papers messily poking out. Someone (not Elspeth, it seemed fair to speculate) had been looking for something in a hurry. I was about to call for my dad but instead walked nearer to the desk. I noticed there was strange goo on the drawer handle that was hanging in strings, so I knelt down to inspect it. I sniffed and the smell reminded me of compost. The goo was dried and had a translucent appearance tinged with a dirty green shine.

'Come upstairs, Becky,' I heard Jess yell.

I ran upstairs to join her; she was in the back room that seemed to be Elspeth's bedroom. It was cold, the window wide open. The view was impressive, and I saw a large bridge nearby. I looked around the room. It was a mess, bedcovers strewn on the floor, a wardrobe open, its contents off their hangers, a chest of drawers, again with its drawers all open. On the floor by the window was a telescope. I stepped nearer to the window and joined my sister. She was studying the mess, looking for answers.

'This is giving me the creeps, Becky,' she said. I looked back at the open window and then noticed a similar goo on the windowsill. Avoiding the ick, I leant out the open window and stared out. I looked down; it was a sheer drop to the garden of the basement flat. I had a wild thought that someone could have climbed up to the window to get in.

'What have you found?' my dad said, as he finally reached us, a little out of breath.

'Whoever attacked Great Aunt Elspeth must have been looking for something,' I said, trying not to sound like a Sunday Night TV detective. 'Her study downstairs has been searched.'

'It's a similar story on the first floor,' my dad said. 'And all the room doors are open, on every floor. Very odd.'

'I wonder what they were looking for,' Jess said.

My dad walked past her and closed the window.

*

Later, in the kitchen, we drank hot chocolate and weird herbal tea and discussed at length what to do.

'Did the lawyer say if anything had been stolen?' asked my sister.

'Nothing that he knew of,' said my dad.

'Did Elspeth have a safe?' asked my mum, stirring her strange smelling tea.

'There was a safe,' said my dad. 'But Elspeth and I emptied it between us after my dad disappeared.'

'Maybe worth a check?' I suggested.

*

My dad pulled back the carpet rug in the back room, next to the kitchen. There was a small cut square in the floor-boards at the centre of the room with a latch and hinges. My father approached it hesitantly but my sister and I beat him to it and knelt either side of it. Jess peered down at the hatch.

'There's a keyhole,' she said. She looked closer at it. 'There seems to be a symbol of crossed swords above it.'

Dad looked at us blankly then pulled the bundle of keys out of his pocket. He sorted through them before he came to one in particular. He lifted it up for us to see. There was a crossed swords symbol on it. 'This is the one.'

He tried it and there was a satisfying click. He opened the hatch up and there before us was a small safe door.

There was a combination dial and a handle. It looked old. 'I wonder...' he said, as he turned the dial, mouthing an old sequence of numbers.

A few minutes later there was a gentle pop and a creak as the safe unlocked. My dad looked up at us both and smiled. He opened the door up and we all gazed inside, my mother looming over the top of us.

'It's a book,' she said.

Like the safe, the book looked ancient. It was bound in crimson leather, quite thick, and worn at the edges. My dad carefully picked it up.

'What is it, Alec?' said my mum.

Sitting up, he flicked through it. 'Seems to be a diary, dating back decades.' He shut it and held it out to my sister and I.

'I seriously doubt anyone would take the time to break in to try and steal an old diary but why don't you two do some investigating?'

Jess looked across the hatch at me. 'You take it. This is your kind of thing,' she said. I took the diary from my dad. He stood up.

'Your mum and I have got things to do. We'll do some tidying and check in with the lawyer. Takeaway for dinner?'

*

Jess put another book back on the shelf, as I read through the diary. Elspeth had spindly handwriting, very neat and stylish. We were in the study, the front room on the second floor. I'd shown my sister the dried goo on the desk drawer handle. 'Now that is weird,' she had said, looking at me with an arched eyebrow. 'Definitely your kind of thing, you nerd.'

We'd discussed a few theories, but none were sensible or made sense. I wondered if the diary might help figure it all out.

I read whilst Jess tidied the study. She said it was a fair trade off and I didn't argue. Once I became accustomed to Elspeth's handwriting, I delved deep into the diary. Started when she was eleven, it seemed the diary had been a gift from her aunt, Millicent Hennessey, the sister of Elspeth's father, Archibald MacBurram. Elspeth's initial entry described Millicent as 'an inspiration, a rare woman of her time.' Millicent was independent, worldly, and much admired by Elspeth.

As I read on, Elspeth detailed how her Aunt Millicent became a mentor to her. Millicent was a naturalist, and a great student of world culture. She taught Elspeth herbology and animal handling and, oddly, how to hunt. There was one grisly passage where Elspeth recounted a hunting trip with Millicent in the Highlands. I flicked through the following years and there was scant mention of Millicent, who had been travelling in the East. In 1933 their relationship was renewed, and Elspeth described how Millicent was 'driven with purpose' to prepare her niece for the years to come. Elspeth documented her feelings on this, unsure of what her aunt had in store for her. By this point I was gripped, and Jess had to throw a book at me to get my attention after I persistently ignored her calls.

'Takeaway is here, idiot,' she said, walking out of the study.

*

I bored them all with what I had found out so far. They were interested but also hungry and it was hard to compete with the delicious curry.

'I never knew she hunted,' said my dad, pleasantly surprised, between mouthfuls.

'Did you ever meet this Millicent?' I asked.

He shook his head. 'She was long dead by the time I was born. My dad wasn't too fond of her so didn't talk about her much. He said Millicent always liked Elspeth more.'

I finished my food, made my excuses, and went back to the study. Thankfully there was a comfy armchair in the corner. I pored over the diary, my mind wandering through Elspeth's world, all the while curious if there was a mystery to be solved here.

There were numerous mentions of Millicent being consulted by many established figures of Edinburgh society, helping with missing persons or items, often where the police had fallen short. Elspeth's training with Millicent continued. Elspeth noted that she became proficient in weapon handling; she particularly enjoyed using the crossbow. By 1935, I was beginning to wonder exactly what it was that Millicent was intent on training Elspeth for.

By 1936 it became clear. Millicent was planning to leave for Spain to help in the fight against Franco. Before she left, Millicent and Elspeth went hunting.

For trolls.

My eyes wide in a mixture of disbelief and doubt, I read and re-read the account of winter 1936. There had been a number of child disappearances in Dean Village, not too far from the house, which had been hushed up by the local constabulary and left unreported by the press. It was a priest who had come to Millicent to enlist her services. Millicent had by this time gained a reputation for solving mysteries of the peculiar kind, with Elspeth at her side as her apprentice.

Millicent and Elspeth began their hunt in Dean Village itself, searching for clues. Millicent eventually picked up a trail that lead them to Miller Row, a lane branching off from the village square by a school. I put the diary down and searched the study, looking for a map of Edinburgh. I found an old one and folded it out on the desk, keen to see the location of these places Elspeth wrote about. Miller Row ran down alongside the Water of Leith, beneath Dean Bridge and ended in another village called Stockbridge. I picked the diary up again.

We scouted during daylight hours. Millicent said that the troll would be sleeping so we would be in no danger. Low winter sun sparkled on the icy path before us. We had not walked far before Millicent pointed and directed my attentions to a leafy overhang, not obviously accessible to those in skirts. 'Troll cave,' she said. 'We return at night in more appropriate attire.'

Elspeth gave account of their return to Miller Row at night. Clad in leather britches, armed with crossbows and short swords, the two women had scaled the rocky outcrop leading up to the cave. I shivered at Elspeth's description of the cave, strewn with bloodied child bones. They had snuck up on the troll and Millicent had unloaded her crossbow through one eye, Elspeth did likewise to the other, blinding the beast, before Millicent clambered up its torso and plunged her sword deep into the troll's heart. Elspeth took great pleasure in describing the priest's face as Millicent had presented him with the decapitated troll's head.

I blinked, mind blown at these revelations, unsure if it was the work of a great fiction writer or what it actually appeared to be. I'd know its truth if I met its author, I concluded.

I barely slept that night. We'd made up beds in the spare rooms on the first floor. On my urging, Dad had locked the door to Elspeth's bedroom. It was a hunch but I did not like the idea of something coming through her bedroom window, slimy claws reaching for our flesh. I read the diary for the next few hours by torchlight until my eyes were sore.

*

I woke to the sound of rattling. At first I thought it was just my imagination, fuelled by my late-night diary reading, but the noise continued. I pulled on my boots, and stepped quietly into the hall, eager to determine where the noise was coming from. The rattling came again, louder, from above. I climbed the stairs as quietly as I could. Another rattle, again above. I climbed the next set of stairs to the third floor and went straight for Elspeth's room. Sure enough, the door handle was rattling. My breathing was fast, my heart thumping in my chest; I had to take a dose of my inhaler.

Mustering some bravery, I approached the door. As I got right up close, the rattling stopped. I must have stared at that door handle for thirty minutes before my sister found me and told me to go back to bed. There was no more rattling.

*

Mr Scarpesian had phoned ahead in the morning to share the good news that Elspeth would be home by mid-afternoon. I was very eager to meet this troll-hunting Great Aunt: I had a lot of questions for her.

Jess and I looked in Elspeth's room, under the pretence of tidying it up ready for her return. We did that, of course, but I had to know if there was any evidence of another visitation. The window was ajar and there was fresh slime on the windowsill. My sister was curious, and I filled her in about the diary: trolls and all. She looked at me like I was mad, and I couldn't blame her. 'It could be a pack of lies,' she said. I nodded.

*

Great Aunt Elspeth was in a wheelchair, brought home by Mr Scarpesian. There was a slightly uncomfortable exchange between Elspeth and my dad. When she saw me, her clear blue eyes seemed to know what I'd read.

We spoke later in her study, when she'd settled back in. I knew she was old in years, well into her nineties, but she seemed youthful, with a keen intelligence that seemed undeterred.

'The responsibility has skipped a generation,' said Elspeth, taking my hand. 'As your father's eldest daughter, you must now take up the mantle.'

I didn't know what to say. I nodded.

Andrew Jamieson has spent many years escaping into fictional worlds as a way of trying to cope with reality. He hasn't fully escaped yet. Creating strange stories and weird worlds are at the core of his writing. He first came across the Literary Salon in his days as a bookseller. He lives in Edinburgh with his family and is a care worker. His debut novel was nominated for the Edinburgh International Book Festival's First Book Award in 2013.

Thank God You're Grown

Catherine Simpson

No more Rainbows, Brownies, Guides
Tiny Tumbles, Tumble Tots, Tiny Teds
No more Ju-jitsu, Karate, Football Skillz for
    Girlz
No more swimming lessons, where teachers bark
    orders
Down echoing pool sides as mums feel their
bones growing old.

Thank God you're grown
No more class mates coming on playdates
'Would little Bryony/Natalie/Chelsea come for
    tea?
What does she eat?
Oh, only chips and nuggets and Jell-O if it's
    yellow
with sprinkles pink and sweet enough to break
    your teeth.'

Thank God you're grown.
No more parents evenings, school concerts,
Sports days, nativity plays
An Encore? Please, God, No.
They grow up too quick, they love to say,

But not for me.
No more Nats and mocks, NABs and NARs
No more Duke of Edinburgh Awards.

Every day I'm glad you're grown
And here to stop me getting old.
From teaching me Twitter, Insta, and emojis,
Facetime, memes, and the perfect selfies
To words for things we never described: cis,
    transgender, non-binary,
You update me, with tighter trousers, shorter
    socks,
Bought not at Tesco but at Topshop.

You teach me class tunes by Bruno Mars
How to join in Carpool Karaoke
How to mix a French martini
How to Keep Up with a Kardashian
How to enjoy the wisdom of will.i.am

But best of all, you teach me to swear:
You chattin' shit? Fuck that noise!
I'm glad you're grown.
And here right now
To stop me fossilising
With your acronyms
I'm LOLing & ROFLing,
Cos being your mum is
Pure. Bang. Tidy.

Catherine Simpson is a novelist, poet, memoir and short story writer. Her novel *Truestory* was published by Sandstone Press in 2015, and her memoir *When I Had a Little Sister* was published by 4th Estate in 2019. Her first attempt at 'networking' was a visit to the Edinburgh Literary Salon at The Wash Bar several years ago when she was too terrified to talk to anyone and ran away. Fortunately, at subsequent Literary Salons her networking skills improved. In 2019, Catherine took part in a Book Week Scotland event for the Literary Salon, talking about memoir writing alongside Ricky Monahan Brown.

It Wouldn't Let Me Forget

Joy Hendry

I nearly forgot
all about the poem
that presented itself to me
a few presents ago
but it came back
picked me up by the scruff
of the jaiket
and lifted me back
to where I present myself now.

What it said to me went like this:

'You are like
Nature in Lockdown
and see in the quiet
and the emptiness
so many chances
so many ways
to emerge into full greenery
out of
the dark undergrowth
our civilisation
has beaten you down
in to.

May be
and it is May
for a yet or two
I can get to know you
presently
in some
now
to come.'

Joy Hendry is re-inventing herself after a lifetime editing *Chapman* magazine, working to change the Scottish cultural scene from appalling neglect in 1970, to the vibrant melting-pot it is now. She is now focussing on her potential, as writer, poet and, above all, just as a person. But, as an incurable 'stirrer', she still does everything she can to enhance the Scotland she loves. She has an Honorary Doctorate from the University of Edinburgh (2005), became one of the Saltire Society's Outstanding Women (2019) and the Scottish Poetry Library gave her its inaugural Outstanding Services to Poetry in Scotland Award in 2020.

She

Sara Sheridan

She
had never seen the sea till she fled.
wave upon wave, endlessly strange.
putting death behind her,
keeping her eyes ahead,
on her life.
and the lives to come.
All of us.

She
landed.
The scent of hops and the sound of drawn out
vowels.
as if she had travelled through time, not place.
Words
raising their voices,
nothing is clear,
and she wonders
Will this ever feel real?
Or will she go on trusting only stolen
moments.
The silent ones.
Water on skin.
A kiss in the darkness.
Two candles on a Friday.

My foremother.
The only she.

Clinging to the sheer precipice of her
determination
that for us,
a twinkle in her eye,
for us,
This will be home.

Sara Sheridan has written more than twenty books and works in both commercial fiction and non-fiction, several of which have made the bestsellers charts. Her work has been shortlisted for the Wilbur Smith, Saltire, and David Hume prizes. She is fascinated by history and its impact on our lives, researching not only in archives but using historical artefacts, art, and the fabric of our built and rural environment. Sara has been a sporadic attendee of the Literary Salon for over a decade. She loves being by the sea, is a voracious reader, and is a campaigner for equality issues (currently supporting the Witches of Scotland campaign).

The Island

Carola Huttmann

That first day on the island was his rebirth. His Renaissance. He'd finally done it. Got away from the ridiculous coercive control of his parents. At 20 years of age. Every time he insisted on his independence a drama the size of World War III erupted, so he had chosen the easy way out. Had gone with the flow, so to speak. Had given into their demands, just to keep the peace. People would see it as weakness, but it was exhausting having to fight his corner every inch of his life. It wasn't something he was proud of, but he refused to harbour feelings of shame or embarrassment.

Albert. Albert Elbers. What kind of name was Albert to give a child in the gloaming between the end of the 20th century and the beginning of the next? What had his parents been thinking? He had stopped trying to fathom their reasoning a long time ago. The bullying at school had been unimaginable. Grandpa, many had called him. For others, he had been Uncle Albert. Some would get physically abusive if he didn't respond to such names. Running up to him, staring into his face so close up he could see the open pores and blackheads and smell the dirt on their skin, chanting 'Albert, Albert, Albert', in a derisive manner, as though his name were an offensive term. Then they would push him around the playground until he fell. If it took more than two minutes before he hit the ground they would trip him up. Either way, there weren't many days when he didn't arrive home from school with scrapes and congealed blood somewhere on his body. His mother rarely managed to hide her disgust at the way he looked. He wasn't sure that she tried very hard, anyway.

'What did you do today to deserve to get beaten up?' she'd say.

When he shrugged and made to go to his room, she would get angry. 'Don't walk away when I'm speaking to you.'

She'd run after him, her court shoes clip clopping across the parquet floor like the hooves of a lively Shetland pony. Grabbing his arm and swinging him around to face her. 'Well?'

He couldn't tell her it was because of the name she and his father had given him that he had to endure his daily thrashings, so he said nothing. Just returned his mother's stare as steadily as he could.

'You should try to defend yourself,' his mother would say, clicking her tongue. *God, how he hated that sound.* 'No wonder you get bullied if you don't show some backbone and stand up for yourself.' That tongue-click again. He could feel his insides curdle and the bile rise in his throat at the sound.

After school he wanted to go to art college in London. His father had laughed in his face and refused to discuss it.

'Show some intelligence for once. How do you think you're going to be able to support yourself with an arts degree, if you even manage to graduate.' A snort, in place of his mother's tongue-click.

'Wearing sandals, putting flowers in your hair and smoking hash is not going to put bread on the table or enable you to take care of your parents in our dotage.'

What an outdated view the old man had. When he had attempted to interrupt his father's tirade, his dad had held up his hand to stop him. 'I'll have no insolence from you, son. You clearly have no idea what it takes to get on in life.'

And so, without consulting him, his father had enrolled him at the Cranfield School of Management on a degree in Business Administration. Located in the historic market town of Bedford, studying there for a couple of years could have been an idyllic prospect. Except it wasn't his choice. And, anyway, he would be expected to carry on living at home commuting daily the forty miles to and from Cambridge where his father worked as Registrar at the University. It was Albert's idea of Hell. And his future was likely to be a succession of tedious office jobs.

When Albert refused to sign the admissions form, the inevitable argument ensued. Their shouting could be heard the length of their middle-class suburban street. Neighbours knocked on their door to ask if Albert and his father were all right. Edward Elbers's chagrin at living their lives so publicly showed itself in his temper at home for the next two months. Albert hated himself for it, but he eventually signed that admissions form, because he was worn down by his parents' constant digs and warnings that he would never make anything of himself. Being savvy in business was the way to get ahead in the 21st century, his father maintained.

It was as he'd imagined. Business administration was as dull as ditch water. Albert did try to apply himself to the topics, he really did. Accounting and Financial

Management (horror of horrors), Business Economics (yuck), Marketing (yawn), Human Resource Management (well, at least it had to do with people), and Employment Law (not as bad as he feared). Almost from the beginning he was plagued by recurrent 'office' nightmares, including: being trapped in his office by an invisible presence, suffocating under stacks of papers, books or office machinery, and jumping from a burning building.

He'd flunked his first end-of-term exams. As soon as he entered the examinations hall and saw the rows of small desks, at which someone of nearly six foot would be extremely uncomfortable, he felt himself float up to the ceiling. Hanging there like a grotesquely oversized angel he looked down on his fellow students as they took their seats. He watched himself walk to a desk in the third row from the front. He tasted nerves, sour on his tongue.

It was not the first time he had been afflicted by stress-related depersonalisation. At school it had been a regular occurrence, but now it felt even more disturbing. Was it due to a semi-conscious desire to do something that would, for once, allow his father to see him in a favourable light? Whatever it was, on terra firma, sitting at his child-sized desk in the third row with the invigilator's gaze hovering over him, his hand shook so badly he struggled to hold his pen. His brain was full of cotton wool and the words he wrote danced in front of his eyes like frisky spring lambs as he fought down his nausea.

Six weeks later his results arrived in the post. His mother opened the envelope while he was at the dentist having his teeth cleaned. He felt the tension in the house as soon as he returned home. His mother met him tight-lipped in the hallway. She pointed towards the living room. His father was pacing the room. He was still wondering what this latest drama was about when his gaze fell on the brown A4 envelope lying on the coffee table. It almost blended with the teak as though trying to hide itself, embarrassed about what it contained. His heart pounding like bush drums, Albert crossed the space from the door to the coffee table, turned the envelope over and looked at the address.

'You opened it even though it's addressed to me.' He spoke as calmly as he could, but inside he was seething. He'd known for weeks the likely outcome of his exams, but now it felt like he'd not been given time to prepare for his parents' onslaught of accusations and blame. Crossing her arms his mother positioned herself by the window as though she expected Albert to climb onto the sill and jump out.

'What happened?' His father spat out the words.

Albert didn't reply. He pulled the sheet of paper from the envelope. Not answering his father would fuel his wrath. Albert knew that. But it wasn't right that his parents should open his mail when he wasn't even in the house. He skimmed the text. *Hell, it could have been worse.* Only one module was Ungraded. The subject was Accounting and Financial Management, so it was not unexpected. He'd even gained a B in Employment Law and a C in the others. But, of course, to his father those grades meant abject failure. In his GCSEs and A-Levels, to his own surprise, he'd managed As and A*s in spite of suffering badly with exam nerves. His father had not seen fit to offer congratulations or praise. He had simply not expected any less of his son, so had not deemed it necessary to waste words that might have boosted Albert's confidence.

When Albert remained silent his father stepped towards him and struck him across the face so hard the sound reverberated off the walls. The violence of it made even his mother gasp.

'You'll resit them, of course,' his father said, in a tone that brooked no argument, before he strode out of the room, They heard him stomping up the stairs. A minute later the door to his father's study slammed shut. After that day father and son did not speak to each other again.

His mother tried to act as mediator for a while, but eventually gave up. His father refused to be drawn into any conversation while his son was in the same room. An uneasy peace reigned in the household. Albert got himself a summer job stacking shelves in a supermarket on the outskirts of Cambridge which his parents were unlikely to visit. The job was mind-numbingly straight-forward which was exactly what he needed at that time. To amuse himself he began making up stories in his head as he went about his tasks. He found people-watching was fun. By noticing what they put into their trolleys he tried to imagine the kind of lives customers led. He began to wonder whether he would make a good writer. It was the first time he'd had any kind of income, and it was a good feeling. His parents did not ask where he went to when he left the house. They probably believed he walked the streets of Cambridge alone, like some saddo, or that he met up with old friends from school. He was grateful that he didn't have to tell them anything.

Then, one day his mother saw him coming out of the bank. Automatically assuming her son was up to no good, her tone was accusatory. 'What were you doing in there?'

'Lovely day,' Albert said, looking up at the clear blue sky. His mother tapped an impatient foot on the pavement.

It reminded him of the sound of a woodpecker's beak tapping at a tree trunk.

'I was paying in a cheque,' Albert said with all the appearance of nonchalance he could muster.

His mother stared, clenching and unclenching her hands held stiffly at her sides. 'You need a bank account for that.'

'I have one,' Albert paused for effect and found he was actually enjoying himself. 'Before you ask, I didn't steal the money. I have a job.'

His mother's eyes grew even wider with surprise and anger. 'Why don't I know about this? Your father will go mad. You're supposed to be studying so you can resit your exams in the autumn. You need to do better this time around.'

Albert remained silent, watching as two red spots appeared on his mother's cheeks and spread down her neck the more she worked herself up.

'You have no idea how to manage money. I'll need to go in and get the details so that I can handle things for you.'

Shaking his head her son blocked the entrance with his body, hoping that no one wanted to enter or exit for the next few minutes.

'I think it's time you and Dad allowed me some independence. You already have me doing everything else you want.'

The slap landed almost exactly where his father's had. The sting of his mother's cuff was acute, because his skin was still tender from the previous one. Tears of pain sprang into his eyes. An elderly couple stared at them as they pushed past Albert to go into the bank.

'Did you see that?' Albert heard the woman say to her husband.

'Hmm… must be mother and son. Fancy hitting…. ' The rest of the man's words were swallowed up by the whooshing of the revolving doors as the couple disappeared through them.

At that moment Albert made a decision. It had been brewing in his mind for a while. Now it was time to stop being a victim and start running his own life.

'Goodbye, Mother,' Albert said. Then, turning on his heel, he walked away.

'Don't you dare walk away from me.' His mother's words followed him, but her son kept on walking.

He slept on a park bench for the next two nights while he thought through his plan. In the morning he showered at work and took up his tasks with a new kind of energy. He had to be careful though. In his head he was already someone different.

Eating take-out pizza or fish and chips for breakfast and dinner was making up for what he considered his lost youth. Like wearing jeans. They were things he had never been allowed to do whilst living at home.

For the umpteenth time he took the scrap of paper out of his pocket on which he'd copied down the details from the small ads notice board in the supermarket where he worked.

ADOPT A CROFT
is a project to rejuvenate the crofting industry
in the 21st century

Tired of the daily rat-race in the city or looking
for a new purpose in life?
Are you up to the challenge of making a
derelict croft habitable again?
Choose between Sutherland on the

Scottish mainland or various remote small
islands in the Outer Hebrides.

You will receive a stipend of £30,000 over three years + an initial set-up
and materials allowance (tbneg)

CONTACT DUNCAN OR EION
AT THE CROFTING COMMISSION
for more information or to apply

Wherever you go there will be views to take your breath away.
Learn new skills. Learn to breathe again.

He mused on how such a notice could have found itself from Scotland all the way down to a store in Cambridge. The world moved in strange ways. On Friday afternoon he handed in his notice at the supermarket. Walking out of the store for the last time, he made straight for the only public phone box left in this part of town.

Duncan, at the Crofting Commission, spoke with a warm lilting voice that made Albert feel safe. There would be no aggressive exchange of words with this man, he felt sure. Frequent pauses between sentences, sometimes even between words, gave the impression that there was all the time in the world to put it to rights. Albert wished he could sound equally laid back and approachable. He was aware that always being on edge with his parents had, over the years, brought a certain hardness to his manner when he dealt with other people.

Duncan didn't seem to think it too much of a problem that Albert didn't have any relevant experience as long as he was willing to work hard and keep long hours. 'You'll learn by trial and error, and there's always neighbours or folk on the internet to help you out. That's what's magic about modern technology. You're never alone unless you want to be.'

Duncan had two options for him. 'I can offer you a croft in Sutherland, about twelve miles north of Helmsdale, or a virtually uninhabited island in the Outer Hebrides.'

Neither meant much to Albert at that point, but the further away he was from his past life the better.

'I'll go for the island,' he said.

'You're a brave man, but it's a good choice. So much potential.' Then Duncan asked Albert his name. 'So I can get the contract sorted,' he said.

'My name is... ' Albert paused while he took a deep breath. 'My name is Smith... Simon Smith.'

There, it was done. He had reinvented himself. It was as easy as that. He had a new identity and a new place to live. A new purpose.

He liked the sound of his new name. Said it under his breath a few times to get used to it. That evening, knowing his parents would both be out – his father at the University's monthly black-tie dinner and his mother at her knitting circle – he went home for the last time. He filled a backpack with some clothes, his laptop, and a few essentials. It felt good to drop his front door key onto the hall table, walk out of the house and slam the door behind him.

After an overnight train journey he was in Edinburgh. He opened a new bank account and arranged for his money to be transferred before his mother had the chance to try and access his funds. He knew it would be the sort of thing she would do and justify it by saying she only wanted to help him manage his affairs.

Another shorter train ride and three ferries brought him to Ensay, named after the Old Norse for Ewe Island. He'd slept in the derelict croft that had lost its roof a long time ago. There was a lot of work to do and many challenges to overcome. But Simon Smith – formerly Albert

Elbers – was confident he could make this new life work. It was his personal Renaissance.

Tomorrow the first animals: sheep, goats, and chickens, as well as all kinds of seeds for planting, would arrive from the neighbouring island. He was ready.

Carola Huttmann holds an MLitt in Scottish Literature from the University of the Highlands and Islands. She won the inaugural George Mackay Brown Short Story Prize in 2013. Passionate about art, literature, and writing, she draws much of her creative inspiration from the richness of landscape, stories, history, and traditions of the Orkney Islands which have been her home since 1995.